To Wally —
see you in the year 2000!
— from Chuck Adams
6/20/96

CALIFORNIA IN THE YEAR 2000

CALIFORNIA

IN THE YEAR

A Look into the Future of the Golden State
as It Approaches the Millennium

CHARLES F. ADAMS

Pacific Books, Publishers
Palo Alto, California

Library of Congress Cataloging-in-Publication Data

Adams, Charles F. (Charles Francis), 1927–
    California in the year 2000 : a look into the future of the Golden State as it approaches the millennium / by Charles F. Adams.
      p.   cm.
    Includes bibliographical references and index.
    ISBN 0-87015-263-7
    1. Economic forecasting—California.   2. California—Economic conditions.   I. Title.   II. Title: California in the year two thousand.
HC107.C2A7   1992
330.9794′001′12—dc20   92-29085
                                                              CIP

Pacific Books, Publishers
P.O. Box 558, Palo Alto, California 94302-0558, U.S.A.

Preface

The very word millennium evokes magic and mystery, fascination and fear, hope and dread. For centuries, mankind has looked forward with a curious mixture of emotions to the momentous time when the calendar will turn on the third thousand years of Christian history.

The millennium has been eagerly anticipated by many philosophers and writers as the beginning of a new era, a time when the age-old problems of human suffering and injustice might come to an end. Pursuers of individual dreams have made the year 2000 a deliberate target in time—when there will be a cure for cancer; when hunger can be abolished; when we can attain a drug-free society; when malaria and leprosy can be expunged; when the problem of acid rain can be eliminated. Mikhail Gorbachev once proclaimed it the time at which the now disdained ruble will be fully convertible to world currencies. Some devout believers in biblical prophecy regard the millennium as the time when a heavenly kingdom will be established on earth.

But the coming of the millennium is not regarded by everyone as an occasion for optimism and renewal. In fact, some believe that it will be a time when humanity and our planet will be at serious risk. Horrifying nightmares of worldwide depression, the devastation of the "greenhouse effect," the blight of deforestation, the threat of nuclear destruction—all are predicted by the pessimists. In fact, predictions of the end of the world have become commonplace as the millennium approaches.

Will the year 2000 mark the beginning of a new golden age of human history, or will it herald an apocalyptic era of chaos and destruction? Probably neither. It is doubtful if either Valhalla or Armageddon is around the corner. The odds are that most of the problems that have haunted mankind for centuries will still be with us to a greater or lesser degree, that none of the worst nightmares will come to pass, that most of man's dreams will still be unrealized. But there can also be no doubt that the year 2000 will be of tremendous importance to the world—and to America—and to California. It is already acting like a powerful magnet on all of us, pulling at our hopes and dreams, shaping our thinking and planning, intensifying our individual visions of where we are going and what we want to be.

How far away is the millennium? Less distant than the year 1980. As of this writing, we are more than a year into the century's last decade. The years that remain may be the most critical in our history, for they will determine the shape of our long-term future as we launch into the next thousand years. The milestone of the millennium is now forcing us to confront our problems, to take stock of where we are, to map out new directions and goals. For California and for Californians, the present decade will be absolutely critical. The questions we ask, the facts we determine, and the answers we find during the years before the millennium will determine whether or not our state will be poised to realize its full potential in the centuries ahead.

How many more people will live in California at the turn of the century? Where will the new arrivals come from? How big will our cities be? What course is our economy likely to take? Which industries will thrive and which will suffer? How many jobs will have to be created? How much will incomes rise? Where will people live? What kinds of housing will be required? What new methods of travel will we need? How safe will Californians be? How will we control crime and criminals? What kind of health care will we have? Can we improve our educational system? Can we protect and improve our environment? Can we assure ourselves of enough water? Will we have new techniques for surviving natural catastrophes? What kind of new lifestyles will develop? How will music and the arts thrive in the environment of the 1990s? How will politics change for Californians?

These are not easy questions. In searching for the answers, I have read the published forecasts of specialists; I have studied official statistics and state documents; I have analyzed computer printouts; I have talked to business leaders and civic planners; I have consulted with educators, scientists, and government officials.

I am especially grateful to:

Anita García-Fante, Office of Public Information, California Department of Water Resources

Diane Dienstein, Information Officer, California Public Utilities Commission

Carole Waggoner, Chief of Program and Policy Division, California Motor Vehicles Department

Janet Wessell, Communications Officer, California Food and Agriculture Department

Lauren Wonder, Public Information Officer, California Department of Aging

Joanne Munso, Administrative Assistant to the Secretary, California Business, Transportation and Housing Agency

Jo Ann Anglin, Information Division, Arts Council of California

Peggy Hudson, Chief, Transportation Planning Division, California Department of Transportation

Gordon Hutchings, Chief of Resource Analysis Branch, California Department of Transportation

William Ahern, Director of Strategic Planning, California Department of Energy

Lance Barnett, Office of Economic Research, California Department of Commerce

Dave Fleming, Department of General Services, Office of the California Senate

Greg Mungano, Executive Director, California World Trade Council

Susan Lange, Public Relations Director, California Department of Education

Hans Johnson, Research Analyst, California Department of Finance

Kris Saslow, Managing Director, Association of California Symphony Directors

Cynthia Scott, Director, California Association of Museums

Ken Larson, Associate Director, California Confederation of the Arts

Robert Steiner, Director, The Foundation Center

Neil Hoffman, President, California College of Arts and Crafts

Charlotte A. Rhea, Research Analyst, Office of the Attorney General of California

Christine May, Public Information Officer, California Department of Corrections

Janice Agee, Special Projects Director, California Department of Education

Toni Welch, Supervisor of Firearms, California Department of Justice

Al Tokuno, Research Analyst, California Employment Development Department

Aviva Bernstein, Director of Marketing, Center for Continuing Study of the California Economy

Raymond Borton, Labor Market Specialist, California Department of Food and Agriculture

Teresa Ishikawa, Office of Airports, California Department of Transportation

Darice Bailey, Information Officer, California Department of Health

Robin Maroze, Research Program Specialist, California Department of Forestry

Sandy Mah, Microcomputer Specialist, California Environmental Protection Agency

Colin Clark, Federal Program Director, California State Library

Mary Sue Ferrell, California Library Association

Dave Kirby, Vice President, California Chamber of Commerce

Frederick Cannon, Vice President and Senior Economist, Bank of America.

A word about the timing of this book. It could have been written and published a year or so earlier, but I made a conscious decision to delay its completion until the final results of the 1990 census were available. The yield of information from this vast federal undertaking was indispensable to a real understanding of where California was at the start of the decade in terms of population, ethnicity, income, locale, age, and lifestyle. And only by knowing for certain where

America and Californians were at that point in time was it possible to make any sensible forecast of where the state and its people might be headed by the end of the decade.

Some of my conclusions are based on hard fact and firm expectation; others are based on probability and likelihood; still others are largely speculative and conjectural. It will be interesting to compare my conclusions at the start of the next century to see how closely they match up with what actually happened in California. There is no possibility that I will be proven accurate in all things, but I hope that none of my forecasts will be too inaccurate and that most of my predictions will be close to the mark.

Here's a suggestion. After you've read *California in the Year 2000*, put it on a shelf where it will be easy to find; then make a note to look through it again at the end of the decade. I hope I won't be too embarrassed!

December 1991   CHARLES F. ADAMS

Contents

List of Figures and Tables

CALIFORNIA IN THE YEAR 2000

As one went to Europe to see the living past, so one must visit California to observe the future.

ALISON LURIE

1

The New Californians

The explosive growth of the population of the state of California is one of the most remarkable phenomena in the history of world civilization. Little more than a hundred and fifty years ago, almost no one lived in California. Except for an undetermined number of native Indians and a scattering of early land-grant settlers, California was essentially uninhabited. You could have traveled hundreds of miles up or down the coast of California without encountering a living soul. Inland, you might have searched for weeks without finding another human being.

Today, only two lifetimes later, there are more than thirty million people living in California. California is easily the most populous of the United States. In fact, more people now live in Orange County than in forty-four of the other states. There are more people in California than in Canada and Mexico combined. There are more Californians than there are Egyptians or Argentineans or Australians.

If California were a nation, it would be the ninth most populous country in the world. The rush to California over this century and a half constitutes a mass migration perhaps unmatched in human history.

THE GOLD RUSH THAT NEVER STOPPED

By the late 1840s, there were a few scraggly villages struggling for existence in the larger bays of the California coast. By 1847, the town that would become San Francisco claimed 850 citizens, and a thin skeleton of streets was laid out against the shore.[1] Five hundred miles to the south, the village Pueblo de Los Angeles was not nearly so prosperous as it slumbered against the slopes of the Santa Monica Mountains. Then all hell broke loose. A sawmill carpenter named James Marshall found a gold nugget on the American River, and when the word spread across America, a great cavalcade of ships and men headed for California. In the month of February 1949 alone, sixty vessels left New York for California, and seventy sailed from Philadelphia and Boston.[2] Fortune-seekers left their farms in the Midwest and fought their way over the mountains in covered wagons.

On September 9, 1850, the day that California was admitted to the Union, 92,000 people lived in California, less than one-half of one percent of the population of the United States. Ten years later, the figure stood at 380,000, an increase of some 400 percent in just one decade.[3] San Francisco itself had grown in breathtaking leaps. One in every three people in all of California, Oregon, and Washington combined lived in San Francisco.

Soon the new arrivals began to fan out down the coast and to push inland. Over the one hundred years between 1860 and 1960, California's population doubled every twenty years on the average. By the turn of the century, it stood at almost 1,500,000; by 1940, it had grown to 7,000,000.[4] In the Depression years of the thirties, many of the migrants to California from the Dust Bowl states of Oklahoma and Texas settled in the central valleys rather than the urban areas.

However, that pattern of migration changed with the advent of World War II. As the state mobilized and industrialized, people from all over America flooded to California in unprecedented numbers. During the decade of 1940–1950, California grew by a full 50 percent; four-fifths of this gain came in the metropolitan areas.

The decade of the fifties saw dramatic growth and development in areas of defense-oriented industry. Santa Clara County doubled in population, as did Santa Barbara County. Orange County grew by more than 100 percent. At the end of that decade, in the year 1960, California passed New York as the most populous of all the United States.[5] California and Californians never looked back.

The population statistics for California in the past century and a half tell the story with sufficient drama all by themselves:

TABLE 1-1
GROWTH OF CALIFORNIA POPULATION

1850	93,000
1860	380,000
1870	560,000
1880	865,000
1890	1,213,000
1900	1,485,000
1910	2,378,000
1920	3,427,000
1930	5,677,000
1940	6,907,000
1950	10,586,000
1960	15,717,000
1970	19,971,000
1980	23,668,000

Source: Bicentennial Edition, *Historical Statistics of the United States,* U.S. Department of Commerce.

The last decade has seen yet another dramatic leap in population growth. Over those past ten years alone, California grew by another 25 percent, with a net increase of 5,806,000 people, more than any other state has ever grown or may ever grow again in a single decade. On September 9, 1990, the number of people living in the state of California passed the 30,000,000 mark.[6]

WHERE DO ALL THE CALIFORNIANS COME FROM?

In the middle of the nineteenth century, of course, California's growth came almost exclusively from migration from the eastern and midwestern United States. But even as early as 1850, there was clear evidence of immigration from other nations. As one historian of early San Francisco noted of the city in that year, "This was a man's town, and there were men of every description—Americans from the east and south, Mexicans and Peruvians, native Indians, escaped Negro slaves, pigtailed Chinamen, Germans, Irishmen and Russians."[7]

In the seventeenth and early eighteenth centuries, what is now California was Spanish territory and after that it became a Mexican province. The Hispanic population has, therefore, always been present, especially in the southern part of the state. One early historian wrote that the town of San Diego "contains between 300 and 400 inhabitants, a large proportion of which are Mexicans."[8]

In the 1860s, the first large groups of Chinese and Japanese immigrants came to California to help build the railroads and to work in the state's burgeoning agriculture. By the end of that decade, the unofficial count of Chinese in the state stood at 60,000.[9] The great majority of them came expecting to return to the Orient when their work contracts were completed, but few of them did.

In the ensuing years, California's growth came from an uncharted combination of foreign immigration, migration from other parts of the United States, and an increase in the rate of births over deaths among Californians themselves.

A constantly increasing life span, combined with a gradually increasing birthrate, accounted for much of the increase in population. To this day, a substantial portion of the state's growth comes from Californians producing Californians. In the 1930s, the crude birthrate—the total number of births divided by the total population—was 13 per 1,000. By 1949, that birthrate had increased to 24.1, and by 1950 it stood at 32.1.[10] It was at this time that the "baby boom" or "population bubble" began—that unusually large number of babies who are now in the prime of man- and womanhood, and who will be in their most productive years at the turn of the century. The "baby boomers" are now having children of their own, creating a second "baby boomlet" in California.

California's growth is now almost evenly divided between natural expansion (that is, births over deaths) and immigration. Yet it is immigration from foreign lands, more than anything else, that is changing the face of California.

One-third of all documented refugees coming to the United States come to California. They tend to be Asiatic immigrants, with some notable exceptions. For instance, during the years of 1987 and 1988, more refugees came to California from the USSR than from any other single nation. Still, the number coming from Southeast Asia continues to dominate the legal California immigration. In the decade of the 1980s, more than half a million Southeast Asian refugees established themselves in California, and the annual immigration increased by 100 percent over those years. Today, sixteen out of every 1,000 Californians is a Southeast Asian.[11] As time goes by, California becomes less and less the western edge of the United States and more and more the eastern edge of the Pacific Rim.

The other major source of state immigration is Mexico, the other Central American countries, and South America. At the present time, one-quarter of all our country's legal immigrants, one-half of all its undocumented immigrants, and 90 percent of all its illegal immigrants from south of the border come to California.[12]

It is almost certain that the number of immigrants coming to California from all areas of the world will increase dramatically in the 1990s. A 1990 change in federal immigration law will allow more foreigners to come to the United States than ever before. The more than one million illegal immigrants granted amnesty and citizenship in 1986 will soon be eligible to bring their parents and children into this country. Refugees seeking political asylum from Eastern Europe, China, and Latin America will flock to the United States in unprecedented numbers. Large numbers of freedom-seekers will come to our country to escape war and poverty, especially in Central America. A significant percentage of all these groups will have California as their destination. The number of immigrants coming to California in the 1990s could increase by as much as 70 percent over the previous decade.

500,000 NEW CALIFORNIANS EVERY YEAR

With a population base of 30,000,000 at the start of this decade, California can look forward to continued growth at an average rate of at least 500,000 annually into the foreseeable future. This forecast is based on reasonable economic prosperity in the state, an era of relative international peace, and basically sound national and state policies.

As our nation and the world look forward to the twenty-first century, California continues to exert a dramatic pull on people everywhere. John Gunther once called California "the most spectacular and most diversified American state,"[13] and its reputation as the embodiment of the American dream remains solidly entrenched in the international consciousness.

The odds are overwhelming that people will continue to flock to California for its sunshine and warmth, its glamour and beauty, its ocean and mountains, its opportunities for employment, its sense of escape and renewal. Despite all the problems that added population will bring, California will remain the "dream destination" for people from all corners of the earth.

It is almost certain that, by the turn of the century, there will be more than 35,000,000 people living in California.

Californians in the year 2000 will comprise one of the most diverse, multicultural, complex, heterogeneous collections of people

FIGURE 1-1
WHERE CALIFORNIA'S GROWTH WILL COME FROM IN THE 1990s

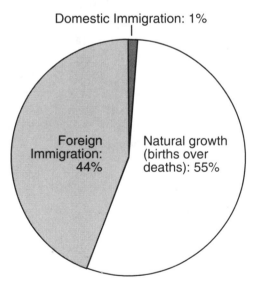

Source: California Department of Finance.

ever gathered together in one place. And because Californians will constitute one out of every eight Americans, their problems and opportunities, their advantages and handicaps, their hopes and despairs will represent the American experience at its fullest.

A LAND OF MINORITIES

Immigration, both legal and illegal, has dramatically altered the human landscape of California in the twentieth century. At the start of this century, California was predominantly white, but even then, the influx of Asians in the northern part of California and the growth of the Hispanic population of the state were clearly visible. It established a trend that will still be accelerating a hundred years later.

In the year 2003, there will cease to be a majority ethnic group in California. Whites will constitute less than half of the population. Hispanics, blacks, Asians, and citizens of other races and nationalities will take their place as members of the first continental state in America made up entirely of minority groupings.

THE GRAYING OF CALIFORNIA

When the United States was founded in the late eighteenth century, the average life span in America was 35 years, and the median age was 16. One hundred years later, the human condition had improved only a little: life expectancy was 40 and the median age was 21.[14]

Although accurate records were not always maintained when California was part of Mexico, it is doubtful that Californians in those times lived that long. By 1900 the life span had improved a little more; it stood at 46.[15] Since that time, a number of developments have extended the human life span and the median age of Californians to a previously unimaginable degree.

Reduced infant mortality, less arduous life-styles, better nutrition, improved communications, and increased urbanization have all

FIGURE 1-2
CALIFORNIA'S PROJECTED POPULATION BY RACE/ETHNICITY
1970–2020

Source: California Department of Finance, Population Research Unit.

played a role in increasing longevity of Californians. The march of medical science, however, has played the dominant role. For example, we no longer have plagues of the magnitude that once decimated the human populace on a fairly routine basis. It is difficult to imagine that as recently as 1917 an influenza epidemic killed 20 million people around the world. The discovery of vaccines, improved personal hygiene, and improved sanitation have made this kind of catastrophe unthinkable. (Even the disastrous AIDS outbreak will claim no more than 10,000 annually in California over the next decade, tragic as that loss is.)

There is no longer any smallpox in California. There is no cholera here. Typhoid and diphtheria are no longer fatal. Tuberculosis, pneumonia, and influenza are no longer major killers. Polio is only a frightening memory. The medical discoveries that have made these miracles possible will continue in the years ahead, helping to extend the life span well beyond its present range.

The average male born in California today can expect to live to the age of 71. The average female born in California today can expect to live to the age of 79. This life expectancy varies somewhat by race and ethnic origin; the life span of blacks is somewhat shorter and those of Asians and Hispanics are somewhat longer. The shortest-lived Californian is the black male, who lives to 65 years of age. The longest-lived Californian is the Hispanic female, who lives to 81 years of age.[16]

The life span of Californians will continue to expand. Within the next three decades, both men and women will live an average of almost three additional years. Again, this enhanced longevity will vary by race.[17]

This increasing life expectancy in California, combined with a declining birthrate, has already raised the median age in California dramatically. In 1985, it grew to 31.3. By the year 2000, it will be 35.4, and by 2020 it will be 36.7.[19] More significantly, it has created a rapidly growing body of senior citizens, the likes of which the state has never seen.

TABLE 1-2
LIFE EXPECTANCY IN CALIFORNIA

	Males		Females	
	1980	2020	1980	2020
White	73	75	79	81
Black	65	70	72	76
Hispanic	76	76	81	82
Asian	75	77	80	81
Average	71	74	79	81

Source: California Department of Finance.

For several decades now, the number of Californians over 65 years of age has exceeded the number of teenagers in California. This trend will continue into and beyond the year 2000.

Over the past twenty years, the number of Californians over the age of 65 has grown at more than twice the rate of the population as a whole. Moreover, the number of Californians living on the far side of the curve is growing with amazing rapidity. More than 60 percent of those over 65 have already celebrated their seventy-fifth birthday, and the fastest-growing segment by far is the over-85 group.[20]

By the turn of the century, there will be more than 3.8 million Californians over the age of 65, and an increasing number of these will be in what is now regarded as the "advanced senior" age group.[21] Every phase of the state's social, economic, cultural, and political life will feel the impact of this growing body of older Californians.

There will also be a dramatic increase in the "chronologically gifted" in California—the number of citizens who attain extremely old age. Not long ago, it was rare to find a person in the state who had reached the century mark. Now Californians, along with Americans everywhere, are reaching the 100-year mark with such frequency that it is considered almost commonplace.

In 1980 there were fewer than a thousand such centenarians known to be living in California. Just five years later there were

FIGURE 1-3

CALIFORNIA'S POPULATION TRENDS FOR AGES 55 +

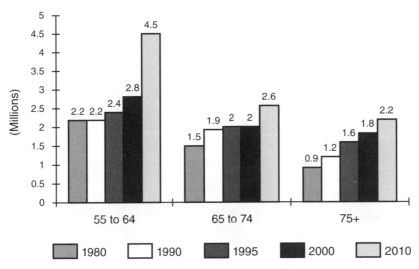

Source: Center for the Continuing Study of the California Economy.

more than 2,500. By the year 2000, there will be more than 12,000 people living in California who are 100 years of age or older.[22]

THE CALIFORNIA BIRTH LEAP

The rate at which Californians replace themselves rose dramatically in the post-World War II period, reaching its peak in the mid-1960s. Birthrates then declined for a decade or so, but are now again climbing dramatically. California birthrates have, in fact, been climbing throughout the 1980s, and now stand at 2.5 births per couple versus just 1.9 for couples in the rest of the United States. From a low of less than 300,000 births in California in 1973, births in the state reached 630,000 in 1991. Almost 15 percent of all babies born in the country are delivered in California![22]

The reproductive rate among Californians is now at one of the highest peaks in recent California history. This high birthrate will continue, and is even likely to grow, between now and the year 2000, partly because of the increasing Hispanic and Asian populations in the state, both of which have substantially above-average fertility rates.

THE CHANGING CALIFORNIA HOUSEHOLD

There are now 10.5 million households within the borders of California, an increase of 1.8 million within the past decade alone. Many of these households differ from the kinds of households most common in California in the past.

The typical California household now contains 2.8 people per residence, well above the national average. California households vary considerably by ethnic classification. The average white, non-Hispanic household, for instance, contains 2.4 persons. The average Hispanic household averages 4.1. The number of adults per California household has risen sharply, possibly because of the cost of housing. The number of California households containing two unrelated adults has grown faster than any other California household type, partly because of the increase in homosexual couples setting up residence. A bare majority of California households today includes a married couple. The recent national census put the number at 52.7 percent.[23]

The number of California households will continue to grow throughout the 1990s, both in number and diversity. By the year 2000, the number of household units in the state will stand at 12.5 million.

THE UNCOUNTED CALIFORNIANS

While official figures at the turn of the century will probably reveal an additional five to six million Californians, the actual number may well be appreciably greater. The principal reason: illegal immigrants from Mexico who daily come across the long California/Mexico border that extends hundreds of miles from the Pacific Ocean to Arizona.

There is no way accurately to measure the number of Mexicans infiltrating into the United States, but informed estimates place the number as high as half a million annually.

Five years after the passage of the Immigration Reform and Control Act, the human flow it was intended to stanch continues unabated. Uncounted thousands of illegals daily run the gauntlet of police patrols, lighted canyons and streams, and volunteer vigilante groups. How many of them succeed and eventually become residents of the state is pure speculation. The 800 U.S. border agents do their best to control the influx, arresting some 1,500 immigrants every night and returning them to their homeland.[24] Many of those return to California without detection and find work in the state's agricultural fields and as domestics in California homes.

Largely as a result of Mexican immigration, the percentage of whites in San Diego County is expected to decline by the end of the century from 74 percent to 60 percent. The number of Hispanics, on the other hand, will rise from 14 percent to 23 percent. It is doubtful if the growth in undocumented aliens can be controlled in the present decade.

Consequently, the official growth in the state of California over these years will represent a serious undercount. Even the census taken in the year 2000 may not accurately reflect the millions of people living in California illegally. The number of "unauthorized Californians" could rise to between three and five million by the year 2000.

WHERE WILL ALL THE PEOPLE GO?

At the present rate and into the foreseeable future, it is estimated that almost two thousand more people will come to California to live every day. By the year 2000, there will be more than two million more California households than there are today.

Where will all these people go? How will they fit into the present population patterns of the Golden State? Which sections of the state will grow the fastest, and which, if any, will dwindle?

First and foremost will be the increasing urbanization of California's population. In a nation that is itself increasingly urban,

California ranks number one among all states in the percentage of its people living in metropolitan areas. The trend in California has been dramatic. At the turn of the last century, only about half of all Californians lived in urban areas, but by 1990 that number increased to an astonishing 92.6 percent.[25] During the present decade, Californians, especially new arrivals to the state, will continue to migrate from the countryside to the cities. By the year 2000, almost 94 percent of all the people in California will reside in the state's almost 8,500 square miles of urban land area.

The cities will boom. Virtually every metropolitan area in California will show growth, varying from gradual to dramatic, over the next decade. Most southern cities on and near the coast will see a real spurt in growth. During this decade the Los Angeles-Orange-Riverside megalopolis will continue to grow until it is virtually one contiguous cityscape.

Los Angeles itself will have the largest absolute growth of any California city for the next thirty years. San Diego will experience continued explosive growth, and Sacramento will expand dramatically in all directions. Together, the San Francisco Bay Area and the Southern California area will represent almost three-quarters of California's total population.

Los Angeles, San Diego, and Orange counties will retain their one, two, and three rankings in population, but San Bernardino and Riverside will surpass Santa Clara County to become the fourth and fifth most populous metropolitan areas in the state.

There will be a number of new towns and cities in California with populations ranging from 20,000 to 40,000 people: Millertown in Fresno County, Rancho San Benito, east of Gilroy, Lakeborough in Stanislaus County, Mountain House, west of Tracy, California Springs in Los Angeles County, Santa Vella in Merced County, Oak Valley in San Bernardino County, Menifee in Riverside County, Tracy Hills in Sacramento County, Eagle River, east of Anderson. None of these towns exists today.

Despite the dramatic future growth of California, one city and county in the state will be reduced in population: San Francisco. San Francisco is on almost everyone's list of the most desirable places to live, but its peninsular location and its severe building restrictions make it impossible to create substantial numbers of new housing units. At the same time, the spectacularly high cost of homes and apartments in the city will continue to drive lower-income families, which traditionally have more children, into surrounding areas.

The result will be that San Francisco's population will continue to shrink very slowly as its residents tend to become higher-income, older, and members of smaller families. In this regard, San Francisco will be unique: all other areas in California will have increases in population between now and the year 2000.

THE COST OF HOUSING WILL FORCE CALIFORNIANS INLAND

Newcomers to California usually suffer from "sticker shock" when they first investigate the housing market. The median-priced house in California costs more than $240,000, and home-buyers must have an annual income of almost $70,000 to qualify for a full mortgage.[26]

By the year 2000, if the recent historic rate of inflation continues, the cost of the average house in California will be more than $350,000.

The cost of housing, however, while severe throughout the state, will vary considerably by area. Generally, houses in the inland, nonurban areas will be considerably lower in cost. For instance, the average residence in the lower desert in Palm Springs will cost much less than one in Los Angeles. The price of a house in the Central Valley will be less than half the cost of one in San Francisco. Because of this differential in housing costs, newcomers will tend to locate inland rather than on the coast. Transportation access will also tend to push California's population away from the coast. As Lance Barnett, director of economic research, California Department of Commerce, says, "If you want to know where California will grow, just look at where the main arterial highways lead. They lead inland."[27]

FIGURE 1-4
PERCENT GROWTH IN POPULATION, 1990–2000

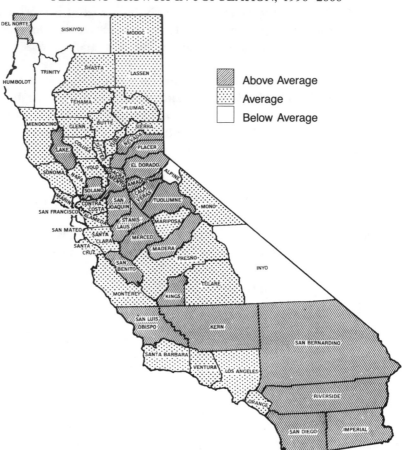

Source: Center for Continuing Study of the California Economy.

The five fastest-growing midsized cities between today and the
end of the century will be Palmdale, with a 23 percent growth rate,
Corona at 13.5 percent, Morena Valley at 12.3 percent, Fontana at
11.5 percent, and Vista at 10 percent. Many smaller cities will
experience even faster growth: California City at 29 percent, Victor-
ville at 28 percent, Perris at 23 percent, and Corcoran at 21 percent.

By the year 2000, California will have nine counties with a population in excess of one million. The Sierra Nevada foothill counties will record an astonishing 120 percent growth over the next thirty years. The fastest-growing counties on a percentage basis will be Riverside and San Bernardino in the Los Angeles Basin; San Benito, Solano, Stanislaus, and San Joaquin near the San Francisco Bay area; Nevada, El Dorado, and Placer near the Sacramento region; and Calaveras, Amador, Madera, Tuolumne, Mariposa, Kern, and San Luis Obispo.

A look at the map of expected growth for all California's counties by the year 2000 shows clearly this development of California in the southern and inland areas.

TABLE 1-3

GROWTH IN POPULATION: TWENTY COUNTIES
WITH LARGEST GAINS, 1990–2000

| County | Population | | |
	1990	1995	2000
Los Angeles	8,863,164	9,475,700	9,961,200
San Diego	2,498,016	2,878,500	3,203,500
San Bernardino	1,418,380	1,757,800	2,044,800
Riverside	1,170,413	1,500,800	1,766,300
Orange	2,410,556	2,661,100	2,854,100
Sacramento	1,041,219	1,213,300	1,368,500
Santa Clara	1,497,577	1,605,100	1,703,900
Fresno	667,490	762,900	855,400
Contra Costa	803,732	893,500	973,500
Kern	543,477	625,600	700,100
Ventura	669,016	746,500	822,300
Alameda	1,279,182	1,358,800	1,420,000
San Joaquin	480,628	546,800	615,600
Solano	340,421	410,100	474,300
Stanislaus	370,522	444,000	494,800
Sonoma	388,222	438,700	488,600
Tulare	311,921	354,400	394,800
San Luis Obispo	217,162	249,200	279,200
Monterey	355,660	388,400	417,800
Santa Barbara	369,608	401,600	429,100

Source: Center for Continuing Study of the California Economy.

The fastest-growing counties in terms of added population will be Los Angeles, San Diego, and San Bernardino, but other counties will show impressive growth spurts as well.

In short, the new Californians, in their growing numbers, their shifting populations, their changing ethnic and cultural characteristics, will dramatically alter the face of California between now and the turn of the century.

BY THE YEAR 2000:

It is almost certain that:

- There will be more than 35,000,000 people living in California.
- One out of every eight Americans will be a Californian.
- There will be 2 million additional families in California.
- California will be on the brink of being a "land of minorities" when no single ethnic group is in the majority.
- The average Californian will be two years older than the average Californian today.
- There will be five times as many widows as widowers in California.

It is very likely that:

- The Hispanic population in California will be the fastest-growing segment in the state.
- Two out of every five babies born in California will be Hispanic.
- Asians will surpass blacks as the second largest minority in California.
- More than 25 percent of all legal immigrants and 90 percent of all illegal immigrants to the United States. will come to California.
- The greatest growth in California's population will be in the inland areas.
- More than 2,000 more people will have come to California every day.
- Twelve Californians will celebrate their one-hundredth birthday every day.

It is entirely possible that:

- California will have twice the population of any other state.
- San Francisco County will have the oldest median age and Merced County will have the youngest.
- California will be more populous than Canada, Mexico, and all of Central America combined.
- Sacramento will be the sixth-largest city in the United States.
- California will have more than a dozen new mailing zip code areas and at least three new telephone area codes.
- Nineteen thousand Californians over the age of 90 will have driver's licenses.

2

The Economic Megastate

Almost from the beginning, California's population growth has been accompanied by a remarkable economic expansion. Although other sections of the nation experienced cycles of growth and decline, boom and bust, California seemed to move steadily ahead, finding one new engine after another to propel its economy.

First came fishing and trapping, then gold and silver mining, then agriculture, then railways, then oil, then movies, then construction—each adding its own impetus to the yeasty mix of California's burgeoning economy. By World War II, California had already become a legendary economic phenomenon, growing and expanding at a rate that left most of America and the world in its wake. With the advent of war, California really took off.

In the late 1940s, the state became, in addition to everything else, America's number one defense and aerospace manufacturer, a position it maintains to this day. Then, some twenty years later, California added yet again to its claim of economic megastar: it became the center of the nation's high-tech and microelectronics industry. Silicon Valley, the Santa Clara Valley in Northern California, was added to El Dorado, Salinas, Long Beach, and Hollywood as a synonym for a major California industry.

Through it all, California had seemed all but impervious to the swoops and vagaries of world economic trends. In the late 1970s and early 1980s, when America wallowed in recession, California simply galloped ahead with its unbeatable combination of advanced agriculture in its valleys, high tech in its hills, and recreation on its shores and in its mountains. Its port cities eagerly took on the task of servicing America's soaring trade with the countries of the Pacific Rim. Its urban centers beckoned to Asian and Mexican immigrants with their history of hard work and low wage expectations. The result was a great leap forward in manufacturing of all kinds— furniture, plastics, electronics, rubber products, clothing, sports equipment, appliances.

During the 1980s, a period of unprecedented expansion in the American economy, California blasted still farther into the lead. In the past decade, California created 3,250,000 new jobs, almost a 30 percent gain on its already sturdy economic base. More significantly, that growth represented an increase that was 50 percent greater than growth in the country as a whole.[1]

California now produces almost 15 percent of America's total gross national product. In manufacturing, in foreign trade, in agriculture, in construction, and in tourism, California ranks number one among all of the United States. In fact, only five nations in the world other than the U.S.—Japan, Germany, France, Britain, Italy—have an economy larger than California's.[2]

As of mid-1990, 531,045 active domestic corporations and another 96,973 nonprofit corporations were doing business in California. In addition, 43,549 foreign corporations are registered in the state. Among them are many of the largest and most profitable companies in the United States. Of the fastest-growing 500 companies in America, 88 are in California.[3]

This remarkable record of sustained economic growth is one of the principal reasons why people from all over the world—to say nothing of Americans from other states—flock to California in such startling numbers. The question, of course, is whether the California economy can sustain the growth that has attracted so many and reward, at the same time, the faith that the new Californians have placed in their new home state. Let's take a look at the reasons for California's economic vitality and the future of some of California's principal industries.

THE SECRET OF CALIFORNIA'S SUCCESS

At the heart of California's economic health is the skill of its workers, managers, and entrepreneurs. On the average, every California worker produces 14 percent more than his or her counterpart in other states. As a result, California's income per person is 16 percent higher than the nation's.[4] Similarly, California's rate of new business formation exceeds the national rate. Minorities and women are far more likely to own their own businesses in California than in other states. In other words, an entrepreneurial spirit and a sustained work ethic are part and parcel of the state's economic success.

California today is moving more and more toward a service-based economy. Less than a quarter of the state's work force is actually engaged in the task of "making things." Finance, insurance, real estate, and the creation, processing, and communication of information are the fastest growing segments of the California megastate.

Research and development expenditures per worker in California are extremely high, a harbinger of strong future success for the state economy. Between 1975 and 1985, this R&D expenditure rose 7.4 percent per year, reaching a total of almost $18 billion in 1985.[5] Such a high rate has not been sustainable in recent years, but even the present rate of 4 percent in R&D growth should sustain technological innovation.

Another measure of the future health of California's economy is the rate at which it generates small businesses, that is, those with 100 or fewer employees. In the recent past, California's rate has been triple that of the national average. The most recent data indicates a net business birthrate (new start-ups over closings) in this category of 3.3 percent a year.[6] During the 1990s this rate should increase to a full 4 percent.

In other words, the entrepreneurial spirit is alive and well in California and likely to remain so in the decades ahead. Even the economic recession of 1991–1992 will not, in the long run, seriously alter the favorable prospects that this high rate of productivity and entrepreneurship portend.

MANUFACTURING: CALIFORNIANS KEEP MAKING THINGS

Despite the growth of the service sector of California's economy, manufacturing continues to be one of the most vigorous and dynamic aspects of the state's economic life. More than 2.2 million Californians earn their livelihood in manufacturing businesses, making California the largest and most important manufacturing state in the United States by a wide margin.[7] The base is diverse: gasoline products, machinery, airplanes, electrical equipment, automobiles, musical instruments, sporting goods, paper products, transportation equipment. California is second only to New York in the production of wearing apparel. The state's fast-growing pharmaceutical industry is a major employer. California's twenty-five largest publicly held companies have aggregate revenues in excess of $140 billion.

California is also a major exporter of manufactured goods. If the state were a sovereign power, it would rank eleventh as an exporter of merchandise, just ahead of Switzerland and slightly behind Hong Kong.[8]

California can be expected to maintain its position in America as the manufacturing superpower. One reason for this is its growing productivity. During the 1980s, when America's manufacturing productivity increased on the average 3.7 percent annually, California's productivity growth was close to 5 percent a year.[9] This rate is competitive with the productivity of such powerhouse nations as Japan and West Germany. In the last decade of the twentieth century, California should remain competitive in world manufacturing. With its favorable geographic position vis-à-vis the Pacific markets, it should continue to thrive, and it may even advance well beyond its present strong position.

AEROSPACE AND DEFENSE

California is the armorer of the United States, with the Department of Defense spending some $60 billion of its $350 billion budget here, about 17 percent of its total expenditures. About $50 billion of that amount goes to weapons development, procurement, manufacture, and maintenance. The most defense-dependent counties are Santa Clara, Inyo, Santa Barbara, Los Angeles, and Orange. Only five California counties have no defense income of any kind.[10]

No one can predict the future of America's defense expenditures, but there is a strong expectation that they will decline during the decade of the 1990s. Forecasts predict a 10-to-30-percent reduction. However, cuts, if any, will be spread over many years by delaying weapons acquisitions, by stretching out weapons deployment, and by allowing inflation to erode real budgets, which should soften any blow to the California economy.

In addition, it is important to note that California is now far less dependent on defense spending than it was several decades ago. In 1970, when substantial cuts materially affected the state, defense spending accounted for 14 percent of the California economy and was responsible for one out of every seven jobs. At the present time, defense spending is only 8 percent of the economy, accounting for just one out of twelve jobs.[11]

It is estimated that a cut of 20 percent in California's defense business now would amount to just three months anticipated growth in the overall California economy.

AGRICULTURE: WHERE CALIFORNIA SHOWS THE WAY

If there is any single segment of the American economy where California clearly dominates, it is agriculture. California stands number one among all states in cash farm crops, exceeding by more than 60 percent its closest competitor, Texas.

California agricultural revenues for 1991 exceeded $18 billion. California produces the majority of all U.S. production of almost sixty crop and livestock commodities, from alfalfa seed to worms. Ninety-five percent of all U.S. wine exports come from California. More than half of all the fresh vegetables grown in the United States are grown in California. Eight of the top ten agricultural counties in the country are in California.[12]

California agriculture is also a major California exporter. Fully 25 percent of all California farmland is in production for the purpose of export, and California farm exports have increased 30 percent in just the past several years. Exports now account for $3.7 billion of California agriculture's total revenue.[13]

Despite five years of drought and a killing freeze at the start of the decade, California's biggest industry remains robust. There will, however, be many changes in the state's agriculture during the 1990s. Without doubt, encroaching urbanization and land development will take some farmland out of production. Recent cold winter weather also means that some retrenching on recently developed farmland in the north will be done. Water continues to be a problem. Allotments to agriculture could drop dramatically if the drought continues, and some marginal and less profitable crops such as corn and beans may be pulled out of production. Cattle ranchers and dairy farmers could be hard hit in the decade because of higher hay prices and lower milk prices.

In general, growers will depend more on wells, deep irrigation, and careful management. Most agricultural operations will adapt to environmental problems and continue to grow and prosper. California farmers started the decade with a minimum of debt and three to five years of good profits.

California agriculture will soon be a $20 billion industry, and the odds are overwhelming that the industry will continue to thrive and prosper for the remainder of the decade.

CONSTRUCTION: SUFFERING NOW, SOARING SOON

One of the mainstays of the California economy over past decades, the construction industry was in the doldrums as the last decade of the twentieth century began. The two principal reasons are, of course, the national recession and the high cost of entry into the California housing market. The median cost of a detached house in the state is well over $200,000; for a condominium it is close to $150,000. This means that less than 40 percent of the heads of households can afford a condominium and only 18 percent a free-standing house. The difficulty of purchasing a California home can be seen from the fact that nationally an income of $33,300 is needed to purchase a medium-priced home, while in California an income of almost $70,000 is required.[14] As of 1989, the sales of single-family homes in California declined for the first time in a number of years. Four of the country's most expensive metropolitan areas in which to buy a home are in California.

TABLE 2-1

MEDIAN HOME PRICES IN MOST EXPENSIVE METRO AREAS

1. Honolulu	$347,000
2. San Francisco	267,500
3. Orange County	240,400
4. Los Angeles	223,000
5. Bergen County, New Jersey	193,600
6. San Diego	189,700

Source: Association of Realtors (as of mid-1991).

As a result of this extremely high cost of housing at a time of economic retrogression, the California housing industry built fewer units in 1990 than in any recent year.

California construction will rebound in the 1990s and reach new heights before the year 2000. The influx of new citizens at a rate of at least half a million a year will put tremendous pressure on housing in the state. The builders of California will respond with a sustained spurt of activity that will carry them well into the next century.

MINING AND MINERAL PRODUCTION: A CALIFORNIA BUSINESS ON THE WANE

It was gold that first turned California into a world mecca. Mining is still an important industry, and California is still preeminent among America's mining states.

Despite California's dominant position in this important industry, a number of problems are looming in this decade. One entire segment of the business is likely simply to disappear: asbestos. The federal government has barred the use of this material for insulation and many other purposes. California will be affected by these restrictions more than other states because of its position as the number one American producer of asbestos.

Oil production in California also faces a problematical future, despite the state's fantastic oil resources and the world demand for oil products. Environmental concerns are limiting drilling opportunities, particularly on offshore sites. Recent court rulings have given California's shore communities and counties the right to restrict and forbid the construction of oil-receiving and -refining operations. In addition, the clamor for alternative power sources for motor cars could reduce the demand for oil in the coming century. Output for both oil and gas in California is down from the high production of earlier years, and no significant new fields have been discovered in recent times. Nineteen percent of all of America's proven oil reserves are in California.[15] The only important new reserves are offshore, and memories of several recent oil spills militate against significant new drilling there.

Oddly enough, the mineral that originally made California famous, gold, is experiencing a real renaissance in California. In the 1980s, gold production in the state soared from 38,000 to almost 450,000 troy ounces.[16] New techniques of mining, higher prices, and foreign investment have encouraged owners to open up new pits and rework old slag heaps.

The future for mining and production of mineral products in California is troubled, not because of limited resources, but because of environmental concerns that will act as roadblocks to future development.

BANKING AND FINANCE: TROUBLED BUT TOUGH

The financial industry in California is facing some problems going into the 1990s, but it is basically tough and resilient and has some clear advantages over its counterpart in other sections of the United States. To begin with, real estate values, which have declined so drastically elsewhere, have seen only modest declines in California. This means that loans to homeowners are not nearly so troubled in California as in most other states.

There are 440 state and national banks in California with almost 4,700 outlets. There are 180 savings and loan associations and 275 chartered credit unions.[17] The savings and loan industry, so troubled nationally, is at least moderately healthy in California. While no new S & Ls have opened in the last four years, fewer than twenty have closed. Combined assets of all these California financial institutions exceed half a trillion dollars.

One other aspect of finance in the state has been absolutely vibrant: venture capital. In 1990, about $900 million in venture capital was placed in California, almost 40 percent of all the venture capital in the United States.[18]

Perhaps the most troubled of California's financial institutions is the insurance business. The passage of Proposition 103 in 1988 has been upheld in the main by the California Supreme Court. This proposition mandates a 20 percent cut in automobile, property, and casualty insurance rates. More than 350 companies write automobile insurance in California, and California ranked third in auto insurance premiums at the time Proposition 103 was passed, with an average premium of $801.[19]

Eighty-six percent of the nation's earthquake insurance is written in California, which is an added source of revenue for California underwriters. Yet, only 20 percent of all California homeowners have earthquake insurance, despite recent rumblings under the state's land and the major Loma Prieta quake of 1989.[20]

Foreign ownership of California's financial institutions is also a matter of major public concern. Four of the ten largest California banks now have substantial offshore ownership. There is no reason to believe, however, that foreign ownership will prove detrimental to California's interests. The availability of Japanese and European capital to California investors could prove a boon to many aspects of the state's economy in the long run. It is estimated, for instance, that Japanese investment during the past decade created almost 70,000 new jobs in California.[22]

During the 1990s, California's financial institutions should remain strong. A growing population base, a diverse economy, stable real estate markets, and a strong entrepreneurial spirit all bode well for the health of the state's banking and finance businesses between now and the year 2000.

TOURISM: AN INDUSTRY LOOKING UP

Most of the people who come to California come not to stay and live but to see and enjoy. Every year, more than 30 million Americans travel to California to visit its cities, see its sights, and drive its highways. In addition, 7 million foreigners annually come as tourists to California, primarily from Mexico, Japan, and Canada. And every year, Californians themselves make more than 75 million trips within their own state for business and pleasure.[23] Together, these travelers fuel one of the major and growing industries of California: tourism. Almost 110 million people travel into, through, and around California every year.

The money they pour into California and California business is staggering: $45 billion. More than half a million California jobs are generated by the state's tourist business, almost 5 percent of all of the state's nonagricultural employment.[24] The payroll attributable to California tourism is put at about $8 billion. California tourism also generates more than $1.6 billion in tax revenues.

Many aspects of the California economy are tourist-dependent, including airlines, hotels, restaurants, bars, retail stores, bus stations, and recreation businesses. These businesses should be heartened by the fact that tourism is on the rise and will continue to prosper in the foreseeable future.

One of California's greatest tourist attractions is its park and recreation areas. The six national parks in the state attract 40 million visitors annually.[25] California also has 12 percent of all the state park and recreation land in the continental United States. Visitors to these state parks are approaching 80 million per year, up from just 20 million some thirty years ago.[26]

With the population of the United States on the rise and with California's population due to increase by half a million a year, tourism into and around the state is destined to boom. The dramatic growth in California tourism may slow somewhat in this decade, but tourism will still grow almost 15 percent by the year 2000. At the turn of the century, tourism will be at least a $65 billion industry in California.

IMPORT/EXPORT

The twenty-first century has been dubbed the Century of the Pacific. And if there is any truth to this appellation, California,

as America's face to the Pacific, is ideally situated to capitalize on the rise of the Pacific Rim.

California is today the leading U.S. exporter of both manufactured and agricultural goods. Its major ports of Los Angeles, San Diego, Long Beach, and San Francisco already constitute the undisputed gateway of the United States to the Pacific. Aggregate trade through all of California's ports increased from less than $9 billion in 1970 to more than $130 billion in 1990, an increase of almost 1,400 percent![27]

More than 80 percent of California's total foreign trade is with Pacific Rim countries, and Japan, not surprisingly, is California's largest foreign trading partner. In all, California annually accounts for about $50 billion in trade with Japan, about half the total of all the other forty-nine states. More than 35 percent of all trade between the United States and Asia passes through California ports. Surprisingly, California's fastest-growing foreign market at the moment is Canada.[28] The two California ports of Los Angeles and Long Beach have surpassed New York ports in number of vessel arrivals.

This relationship between the Pacific countries and California as major favored trading partners will grow throughout the decade to the point where California might well be considered a Pacific Rim country as far as international business is considered.

A NEW BUSINESS RELATIONSHIP WITH MEXICO

Despite sharing an immense common border with Mexico, the California economy did not really interface economically with that of its southern neighbor until a decade ago. Since that time, however, the policies of Mexico and the United States have greatly encouraged economic integration, and at an accelerating pace.

First, the Mexican government lowered trade barriers. Then, in 1985, the *maquiladora* program resulted in the location of nontariff manufacturing plants on the border. Now the North American Free Trade Agreement is expected to be consummated. The present timetable calls for both houses of Congress to vote on such an agreement with Mexico in May of 1993.

If this agreement is put into effect, the virtual economic integration of California and Mexico will dramatically boost the region's trade, output, and employment. Trade between Mexico and California will mushroom at a rate of 10 percent annually through the rest of the 1990s. California, which currently runs a small surplus with Mexico, will see this surplus grow though the decade as a result of increasingly attractive investment opportunities in Mexico. The agreement should also boost Mexican manufacturing jobs, California service jobs, and other foreign investment in Mexico.

One other benefit of the agreement will be to reduce the wage differential between the Mexican and Californian economies over time, a change that will eventually reduce the pressure of illegal Mexican immigration to California.

In the broadest sense, the North American Free Trade Agreement, assuming its approval by Mexico and its ratification by Congress in 1993, will eventually create the world's largest market, consisting of Mexico, Canada, and the United States. This market is actually larger than the European Economic Community, which should come fully into being in 1992. The benefits to California will be immense in terms of job-creation, international trade, and overall economic growth.

MOVIES: THE GLITTER IN THE CALIFORNIA ECONOMY

The business of making motion pictures has been a California enterprise almost from the beginning. Today, film making is a full-blown industry making a major contribution to the state economy. Every year, more than half of the some 400 movies made in America are made in California. The principal producers are Buena Vista, Paramount, Fox, Warner Brothers, Columbia, MGM/UA, and Universal.

According to the California Film Commission, approximately 118,000 people are directly employed in the state's film industry and another 116,000 are indirectly employed. Feature films, television shows, and television commercials produced in California generate almost $5 billion in revenues, representing 62 percent of all such revenues in the United States. The annual payroll of Californians working in both film production and film distribution represents another $3 billion.[30]

The number of motion picture theater screens in California has increased dramatically over the past decade—from 1,600 to more than 2,500 at present. There is one exception to this growth: drive-ins, which have dwindled from 275 to fewer than 150 over that same period.[31]

The purchase of California film corporations in recent years has disquieted many observers. Australian interests bought MGM/United Artists and 20th Century-Fox; the British picked up MTM Entertainment; the Italians acquired Canon; and the Japanese purchased Universal and Columbia.

By and large, fears that foreign influence will dim the luster of this major California industry are false. On the contrary, the infusion of major foreign capital, combined with California skills and talents, means that the film industry will prosper as never before in the 1990s. More films will be produced, revenues will sharply increase, and American dominance of the world market will be even stronger by the end of the century.

SAY "GOODBYE" TO AUTOMOBILE PRODUCTION

By the summer of 1992, General Motors will have closed its Van Nuys assembly plant. The 100-acre plant, GM's only plant manufacturing Camaro and Firebird cars, will cease operations after the completion of the 1992-model run. The closure will mean the loss of 3,500 high-paying jobs in Southern California. More importantly, it signals the next-to-last nail in the coffin of what was once a flourishing industry in California.

Just two decades ago, it seemed that California, with its huge car market, was destined to be a major producer of motor cars as well. But with the demise of the Van Nuys plant, all but one of the California automobile production plants will have been closed and operations shipped outside the state. The General Motors Fremont plant, owned jointly with the Japanese, is the last survivor.

By the year 2000, car production may cease altogether in California, a victim of high production costs and the still-growing popularity of Japanese and other foreign-made cars in the West Coast market.

CALIFORNIA'S UNDERGROUND ECONOMY

As impressive as the official numbers are that describe the California economy, it is almost certain that they are understated. In reality, the California economy is even more robust than the official record indicates. It has been estimated that at least 10 percent of the state's economy is "off the books." Unregistered immigrants with paying jobs, citizens who deal in barter rather than in financial exchange, income that goes unreported for either legitimate or illegitimate reasons, "cottage industries" in private homes, garage and back-alley factories, companies that for one reason or another do not report all of their earnings—all of these are part of California's underground economy.

This unofficial state product could already be as high as $70 to $90 billion annually. If this is true, then the actual size of the California economy could already be $820 billion. Because of higher taxes and the difficulty of enforcing labor laws, California's underground economy will grow during the 1990s at an even faster rate than the official economy, possibly adding as much as 15 percent to the overall total.

SAN FRANCISCO VS. LOS ANGELES: A BATTLE LONG OVER

The century-long argument as to which of California's two best-known cities was the true western gateway city ended several decades ago.

San Francisco, hampered by geography, union-paralyzed port facilities, and a city government widely perceived as anti-business, lost the battle to its southern rival years ago with hardly a whimper. The past, present, and future all favor Los

Angeles as the center of economic development and international trade.

- In 1989, the equivalent of 2,500,000 containers passed through the ports of Los Angeles and Long Beach, her immediate neighbor to the south. The port of San Francisco handled just 114,000.[31]
- The center of banking and finance in California has been gradually moving to Los Angeles for several decades.
- Foreign companies selecting a California base now almost invariably look south. Orange County is already home to more than 300 American headquarters of Japanese companies. Nine of the Pacific's largest car companies have their American headquarters in Los Angeles.[32]
- Los Angeles last year exported $62.7 billion in goods, San Francisco just $27.2 billion. For that same period, Los Angeles imported $38.5 billion, San Francisco only $21.4 billion.[33] This disparity has been growing year by year, a trend that will continue into the foreseeable future.
- San Francisco is the only major Pacific Rim city that lacks a world trade center for freight forwarders, customs brokers, and financiers. When the $550 million World Trade Center opened in 1989 in Los Angeles, the disparity between the rival cities was compounded.
- In the past twenty years, almost a dozen foreign nations have moved their consulates from San Francisco to Los Angeles in recognition of that city's economic supremacy.

In fact, San Francisco is very quickly losing its international business edge to its less glamorous neighbor down the peninsula, San Jose. Measuring on a per-capita basis, Silicon Valley, with San Jose as its base, is the second-largest value-added exporting region in the United States. San Jose's City Hall has a major Center for International Trade and Development that actively solicits business from Pacific Rim countries and companies. Osaka has located a trade office in San Jose, and the Japan Society of Northern California has recently moved its headquarters there. The recent census confirmed that San Jose has officially passed San Francisco in population.

The decade of the 1990s will see Los Angeles continue to lengthen and strengthen its lead over San Francisco as California's recognized gateway city to the Pacific. The two southern ports of Los Angeles and Long Beach have formed an alliance aimed at doubling their container capacity by the year 2020, a goal they will probably realize.

San Francisco will continue to decline as an important port city and as a center of international business. By the year 2000, it will be supplanted by San Jose as the business capital of Northern California.

NEW MOVE TO THE METRIC SYSTEM

Today, more than fifteen years after President Ford signed the Metric Conversion Act, Californians are no closer to adopting the international system than most Americans. However, that could change dramatically in this decade. The need for business to go metric is paramount. By the end of 1992, the U.S. government's thirty-seven largest agencies and departments will have converted to metric for all procurement and business activities. California's equivalent departments will, of necessity, follow suit, and the ripple effect will be enormous throughout the state. The impact will be felt in supermarkets, department stores, and packaging of all kinds. Major U.S. carmakers and drug companies have already gone metric, and other businesses will follow throughout the 1990s at an ever-accelerating rate.

Californians, like it or not, will start using the metric system out of necessity by the year 2000—and almost all California business will go metric.

THE PROBLEMS

Despite the many reasons for optimism about California's long-range economic future, several roadblocks could keep the state from realizing its full potential at the millennium.

- Defense cuts now on the books following the build-up of the 1980s could cost Southern California thousands of jobs. Defense spending accounts for 8 percent of the state's economy, and any further downturn in defense needs could send such major California contractors as McDonnell Douglas and Lockheed into a tailspin. A number of important businesses have already begun to transfer defense work out of state to lower-cost locations.
- The rising costs of environmental legislation could drive many businesses out of the state or prevent out-of-state businesses from expanding into California. If air quality regulations and environmentally based taxes become too severe, more and more low-wage California-based manufacturing could be driven south across the Mexican border.
- The cost of housing in California could discourage the migration of out-of-state business into California. More and more companies considering a transfer of operations and personnel to the West Coast are becoming aware of the hardship that the housing market works on their personnel. The median price of a home in California has increased 700 percent since 1970, almost twice the national rate.[34] Often executives are simply unable to make the move because of the differential in the cost of living.
- The long-term availability of energy and water in California poses a real threat to industry in the state. California's nuclear energy capability has been effectively crippled, and a succession of drought years has brought the long-term availability of adequate water supplies into question.
- The decline of the educational system in California could mean a future shortage of skilled, literate workers to fill the management jobs in what is becoming California's fastest-growing segment: the medium-wage white collar service jobs in the state's shops and offices.

None of these problems, however, is serious enough to cripple or stall for long the overall economic growth of California in the 1990s or in the early part of the twenty-first century. Despite the recessionary period at the start of the decade, an inherent impetus for growth and development in the major sectors of the state's economy will carry it well beyond the millennium.

THE MEGASTATE AT THE TURN OF THE CENTURY

Despite a slow start, the economy of California will continue to grow throughout the 1990s, probably at a rate rivaling that of its development over the past three decades. Despite some shift in the emphasis of its basic mix of industries, California's fundamental reliance on its existing businesses will endure.

California's annual growth rate will average 3.5 percent over the intervening years. California will create 284,000 new jobs annually between 1992 and the year 2000. California's gross annual product for all goods and services of $730 billion at the start of the decade will pass the $1 trillion mark before the mid-1990s and could grow to $1.3 trillion by the year 2000. The state's economy in relationship to the economies of other nations will fluctuate with the value of the dollar, but will remain one of the top ten in the world.

BY THE YEAR 2000:

It is almost certain that:

- The California economy will have averaged an annual market growth of 3 percent for the decade.
- Three out of every four working Californians will be employed, not in agriculture or manufacturing, but in the service sector.
- More than 750,000 corporations will be active in California.
- One hundred of America's 500 fastest-growing companies will be operating in California.
- The number of businesses catering to the Hispanic market in California will multiply dramatically.
- Seagate Technology will build a new $50 million factory near Dublin that will employ almost 1,500 people.
- California will be the tenth-largest exporter of manufactured goods in the world.
- California's Department of Defense spending will drop below $40 billion.
- San Diego will feature a whole new skyline including a 40-story Hyatt Regency, a twin 41-story condominium called One Harbor

Drive, a 50-story tower complex called Roger Morris Place, and a new 30-story office-hotel complex called Emerald Shapery Center.

- Home construction in California will increase and commercial construction will decline.
- The Los Angeles-Long Beach and the Anaheim-Santa Ana metropolitan areas will lead the nation in job growth.
- There will be more mergers of banks and financial institutions in the state.
- Tourism in the state will exceed $70 billion in revenue.
- Trade between Mexico and California will increase dramatically.

It is very likely that:

- The California market will have expanded by more than one-third in real dollars.
- San Diego County will have the twenty-fifth-largest economy in the world.
- The underground economy of the state will grow as taxes increase, possibly reaching $100 billion.
- Foreign trade will account for 25 percent of California's total gross state product.
- There will be 200,000 fewer Californians working in the defense industry.
- Newport Beach will boast a new 450-room coastal hotel built by Hyatt Corporation, part of a new Irvine Coast development that will include 2,600 new homes and several golf courses.
- San Diego will be eighth nationally in job creation; San Jose will be tenth.
- More than half of all revenues from California films and records will be earned in foreign countries.
- The I-680 corridor in Contra Costa County will be one of the hottest new economic regions in California.
- California's economy will outdistance that of Italy, of France, and of all the Scandinavian countries combined.

It is even possible that:

- Californians will reluctantly be using the metric system in almost all business conversations.

- A new office and retail center will be built on sixteen acres of downtown Anaheim at a cost of $200 million.
- California will have less than half the number of banks it has today.
- Downtown San Jose will sprout a number of major new hotels, including a new 15-story Hilton Hotel near the convention center.
- The University of Southern California will build a $100 million commercial project near its campus with office, retail, and hotel space.
- A dozen new skyscrapers will be added to the skyline of downtown Los Angeles.
- More than 1,000 new shopping malls will be built in California.
- California will be the fourth leading economic power, surpassed only by the United States, Japan, and Germany.

Californians at Work

People will move to California in the 1990s for a variety of reasons. But the one incentive that will be paramount for those coming from other states, as well as those coming from other nations, will be the same: a *job*. California has long been known, even in the toughest of times, as a place where a man or a woman could expect to find work.

Despite the economic downturn at the start of this decade, California's overall reputation as a good workplace will no doubt continue into the next century. But the state's economy will be hard pressed to generate the number of jobs that will be necessary to satisfy both its existing residents and its new citizenry.

MORE AND MORE CALIFORNIANS WILL BE WORKING

In 1990, 65 percent of the total population of California had a job of some kind, an increase from 61 percent just a decade earlier.[1] There are a variety of reasons for this. The economy was healthy through most of 1990. The number of women in the work force grew dramatically. And many more senior citizens elected to continue work or to take part-time jobs to augment their income.

All of these trends are likely to continue. The percentage of Californians in the work force could approach 70 percent by the year 2000, especially if the birthrate declines as the population becomes older.

JOB GENERATION: THE STATE'S NUMBER ONE PRIORITY

If California is to keep pace in its ability to provide work for its citizens, both old and new, it will have to create new jobs at an unprecedented rate. The Department of Commerce estimates that in order to provide sufficient work opportunities for its citizens, California will have to create one out of every six jobs in the United States between now and the year 2000.[2]

The California "job machine" in the 1980s produced at a rate that was 50 percent higher than the rate for the rest of the nation. The growth of high-tech industries in the early part of the 1980s was a major factor, but less publicized growth also took place in basic manufacturing, especially in the furniture, apparel, machinery, and chemical industries. The "job machine" will have to keep working with renewed vigor in this decade just to keep even with demand.

The Commerce Department has put the number of new jobs required in California during the rest of the decade at 3.4 million, which would be an increase of 21.4 percent between its base year of 1988 and the end of the century.[3] But this figure is probably minimal because it is based on an estimated increase in California population lower than most estimates. If, however, it proves to be accurate, then the number of jobs in California in the year 2000 will stand at 19,070,000.

WHERE WILL 3,500,000 NEW JOBS COME FROM?

It is difficult to look ahead with real specificity to the end of the century, but the California Employment Development Department has projected an overall economic job trend by business category that shows clearly that the growth will be in services. From paralegal (#1) to lecturer (#20), the expansion in employment opportunities will be in Californians providing services to other Californians.

WHERE WILL THE JOBS BE FOUND?

Jobs will grow at a faster rate in almost every area in California between now and the year 2000. The number one leader in new jobs among California metropolitan areas for the next fifteen years will be the Los Angeles area, which will create nearly one in every two new jobs in the state. The Sacramento region will have the highest actual growth in job rate, with an annual gain of almost 3 percent, or some 23,000 new jobs per year. Close on its heels will be the San Diego area with a 2.8 percent annual job growth rate, followed by the San Francisco Bay Area, which will account for only one in every five new California jobs.

Clearly, most of the actual job creation will be in the south. Together, the Los Angeles-Long Beach megalopolis, plus the Anaheim-Santa Ana and San Diego metropolitan areas, will generate more new jobs than the next ten metro areas combined.

TABLE 3-1

CALIFORNIA'S FASTEST-GROWING OCCUPATIONS, 1987–2000

Occupation	1987	2000	Number of New Jobs	Percent Change
Paralegal Personnel	10,910	22,900	11,990	109.9%
Tax Preparers	4,290	8,290	4,000	93.2%
Data Processing Equip. Repairers	13,880	26,630	12,750	91.9%
Photoengraving, Litho. Mach. Operators	1,010	1,850	840	83.2%
Employee Interviewers—Private or Pub.	6,080	11,130	5,050	83.1%
Systems Analysts—Elec. Data Proc.	49,190	89,360	40,170	81.7%
Home Health Aides	11,800	21,400	9,600	81.4%
Computer Programmers	48,220	86,320	38,100	79.0%
Medical Records Techni. & Technol.	5,540	9,760	4,220	76.2%
Law Clerks	3,210	5,650	2,440	76.0%
Computer Programmer Aides	13,770	23,950	10,180	73.9%
Physical Therapists	6,780	11,730	4,950	73.0%
Data Keyers—Composing	1,860	3,170	1,310	70.4%
Safety Engineers—except Mining	3,570	6,040	2,470	69.2%
Social Welfare Service Aides	2,780	4,670	1,890	68.0%
Elect. and Electronic Engineers	80,850	135,740	54,890	67.9%
Offset Lithographic Press Setters	8,780	14,690	5,910	67.3%
Credit Analysts	4,080	6,760	2,680	65.7%
Lawyers	45,380	74,990	29,610	65.2%
Lecturers	3,250	5,340	2,090	64.3%
Nursery Workers	2,520	4,120	1,600	63.5%
Physical Therapy Assistants	4,100	6,660	2,560	62.4%
Occupational Therapists	3,180	5,160	1,980	62.3%
Electrical, Electronic Eng. Techs.	61,630	99,970	38,340	62.2%
Radiological Technicians	6,240	10,110	3,870	62.0%

Source: California Employment Development Department.

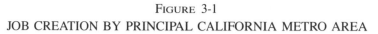

FIGURE 3-1

JOB CREATION BY PRINCIPAL CALIFORNIA METRO AREA

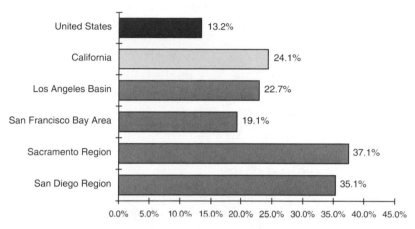

Source: Center for Continuing Study of the California Economy.

HOW MUCH MONEY WILL CALIFORNIANS MAKE?

Californians already earn more money than most U.S. citizens. The most recent calculations show that the average household income for all California households is more than $44,000.[4] On the basis of nothing more than an average inflation rate, this figure should rise to over $60,000 by the year 2000.

However, income per worker will continue to vary in California by region. In the most recently available figures for annual pay by area in California, for instance, average income varied from the highest figures in San Jose and San Francisco to the lowest pay in Visalia-Tulare-Porterville and Chico. But, in general, income throughout California averaged 14.5 percent higher than income for the U.S. as a whole.

California incomes will continue to rise through the 1990s just as they have every year for the past three decades. The increase in California's total personal income, as well as in wages and salaries, will increase through the decade at a slightly lower rate than it did during the 1970s and 1980s. Income from property ownership will also increase more slowly. Dividend income will grow at a slightly slower pace. Farm income, on the other hand, will show a genuine spurt through the decade.

Per-capita income for Californians, which has shown excellent increases for the past thirty years, now stands at about $20,000, more than 10 percent higher than the national average.[6]

By the year 2000, California's total personal income will be almost $1,300 billion. Per-capita income will rise to $29,000,which will be just 5 percent higher than the national average. Average household income will exceed $60,000.

EIGHT WINNING CALIFORNIA CITIES

Eight metropolitan areas in California will be among the fastest growing in the United States in terms of both total and per-capita income. Employment in these areas will also be among the fastest growing in the U.S. These California cities with the best prospects are:

TABLE 3-2

PERCENT GROWTH OF CALIFORNIA CITIES BY THE YEAR 2000

	Total Inome	Employees	Per-Capita Income
Riverside	40.8%	25.2%	13.7%
San Diego	38.8	26.0	13.8
Sacramento	38.6	26.8	13.6
Anaheim	36.5	29.2	13.6
Oakland	33.4	22.0	15.8
San Jose	32.3	20.7	16.9
Los Angeles	29.5	17.2	12.7
San Francisco	25.9	16.9	16.2

Source: U.S. Department of Commerce.

At the start of the next century, one California megalopolis, Los Angeles-Riverside-Anaheim, will top all metro areas in the United States in economic growth. The San Francisco-Oakland-San Jose megalopolis will not be far behind. In terms of income growth, Riverside will be fourth among the nation's cities, behind Orlando, Phoenix, and West Palm Beach.

WHICH INDUSTRIES WILL FLOURISH?

Not all aspects of the California economy, of course, will share equally in the growth of the 1990s, and job generation will be more pronounced in some business areas than others. Agriculture, while still a major force in California's future, will probably not produce the number of additional jobs that its prominence might suggest. To begin with, it is not a labor-intensive business for its volume, and future mechanization will make it even less so. Almost all of the service industries, as previously stated, will produce dramatic new job opportunities, as will the transportation industry. One other industry, impressive now in its size, will also grow substantially before the end of the century: government.

TABLE 3-3

WHERE THE JOBS HAVE BEEN—ARE—AND WILL BE: CALIFORNIA LABOR MARKET AND EMPLOYMENT (IN THOUSANDS)

					Average Annual % Change		
	1979	*1989*	*1995*	*2000*	*1970s*	*1980s*	*1990s*
Labor force	11,268	14,518	16,273	17,800	3.0	2.6	1.9
Civilian employment	10,566	13,780	15,459	16,928	2.8	2.7	1.9
Unemployment	702	737	814	872	6.6	0.5	1.5
Unemployment rate	6.2%	5.1%	5.0%	4.9%			
Nonfarm employment	9,665	12,575	14,500	16,030	3.4	2.7	2.2
Mining	39	40	39	40	1.9	0.2	-0.2
Construction	449	647	708	766	3.7	3.7	1.5
Manufacturing	2,013	2,165	2,244	2,358	1.9	0.7	0.8
Durable goods	1,369	1,447	1,473	1,556	1.8	0.6	0.7
Nondurable goods	644	718	771	802	2.1	1.1	1.0
Transportation, Utility	535	604	641	664	1.3	1.2	0.9
Trade	2,224	2,984	3,460	3,766	4.1	3.0	2.1
Wholesale trade	564	768	875	952	4.1	3.1	2.0
Retail trade	1,660	2,216	2,585	2,814	4.0	2.9	2.2
Finance	596	835	951	1,050	5.2	3.4	2.1
Services	2,075	3,298	4,322	5,031	5.4	4.7	3.9
Government	1,735	2,002	2,210	2,391	2.2	1.4	1.6
Federal	323	357	366	377	-0.4	1.0	0.5
State and local	1,412	1,645	1,842	2,014	3.0	1.5	1.9

Source: California Employment Development Department and California Department of Finance.

NOT EVERYONE IN CALIFORNIA WILL BE WORKING

At the present time, more than a million persons in the labor market in California are unemployed. It is impossible to predict what this number will be at the end of the century, but if the percentage of the total work force remains constant, the number will rise to about 1,175,000. If, however, the Department of Finance figure in the table above is accurate, only 772,000 will be out of work. The overall health of the economy at that time will be the determining factor.

THE CHANGING FACE OF THE CALIFORNIA WORK FORCE

At the start of this decade, California's work force numbered about 14.7 million, an increase of over 3 million during the 1980s.[7] The age and ethnic profile of this work force have changed dramatically during this decade and it will continue to change over the decade of the 1990s. At the present time, the California labor pool is male, white, and middle-aged.[8]

Almost 55 percent of the state's workers are male. This percentage is down considerably from years past, owing primarily to the entrance of large numbers of women into the labor market.

Fully 60 percent of California's workers are Caucasian but here again, the number is considerably reduced. There are now 3.5 million workers of Hispanic origin and 1.6 million of Asian descent in California.

More than 2 million workers in the 35–54 age group were added to the California work force in the 1980s, and this age group now represents 43.5 percent of the total. Younger workers (16–24) declined by 200,000, and older workers (54+) stayed about the same.

The year 2000 will see some major changes in this work force mix. By the end of this decade, more than 80 percent of California's total labor force growth will be Hispanic and Asian. Whites will represent a significantly declining share of the labor pool, and blacks will remain about the same.

TABLE 3-4

CALIFORNIA LABOR FORCE BY ETHNIC GROUP,
1990–2000 (IN THOUSANDS)

	Total 1990–2000		Growth 1990–2000	% of Total 1990–2000	
White	8,662	9,008	346	58.9%	51.0%
Hispanic	3,516	5,176	1,640	23.9%	29.3%
Asian (and others)	1,568	2,382	816	10.7%	13.5%
Black	971	1,093	122	6.6%	6.2%

Source: Center for Continuing Study of the California Economy.

THE DECLINE OF UNIONISM

In the years following World War II, labor unions in California seemed firmly entrenched as a dominant factor in the workplace. By 1950, more than 40 percent of all nonagricultural workers and almost 55 percent of all manufacturing employees were members of organized labor. Since that time, however, labor unions have played a declining role in California work life. The absolute numbers of union members have increased since that time from slightly more than a million and a half to more than two and a quarter million. But as a percentage of all California workers, union membership has been more than cut in half.[9]

This decline is almost certain to continue in coming years. The rise of individualism in the workplace, government regulation of business and its relationship with employees, and the growth of small, traditionally nonunion categories of business all militate against effective union organization. Manufacturing, the traditional stronghold of union membership, is gradually giving way in importance to more service-oriented industries where unionism plays a less effective role.

By the year 2000, less than 15 percent of California workers will be members of labor unions.

THE MULTIPLE-INCOME FAMILIES IN CALIFORNIA

The entrance of California women into the work force over the past several decades has been dramatic. In 1970, for instance, the overwhelming majority of all workers were male. By 1990, that huge majority had declined to slightly more than half. Because so many of the women who entered the labor market were married, the number of multiple-income families in California also grew dramatically. Approximately half of all the income gains per household in the 1980s resulted from this growth in two-earner families.[10]

This trend will, however, level off dramatically in the 1990s. During this decade, the increase in the number of workers per household will be only one-sixth what it was in the 1980s, even though the absolute percentage will grow.

The reason for this is that most people both willing and able to work are already on the job. This means, in turn, that the increases in income for California homes will have to come from real wage increases rather than from second, or additional, paychecks.

WHAT THINGS WILL COST IN CALIFORNIA

Higher incomes and bigger paychecks in the year 2000 will not be the bonanza they seem to be at first glance. Quite simply, things will cost more, from housing, to traveling, to eating, to vacationing. The decline in the value of the dollar is certainly nothing new, as can be seen from this look at what has happened to its purchasing power over the past forty years:

TABLE 3-5
PURCHASING POWER OF THE DOLLAR
(1967 = $1.00)

Year	United States	California
1950	1.27	1.45
1960	1.07	1.13
1967	1.00	1.00
1970	.91	.87
1980	.41	.40
1982	.35	.34
1984	.32	.32
1986	.31	.30
1987	.30	.28
1989	.28	.27
1991	.26	.25

Source: Consumer Price Index, California Department of Finance.

In brief, the dollar of 1967 is worth less than a quarter today. What this bodes for the future is difficult to say. However, if the recent rate of inflation continues for the rest of the decade, it is possible to calculate what certain items of importance to Californians will cost in the year 2000.

Here, on the basis of recent inflation rates and other probabilities, is what Californians can look forward to by the end of the century.

The Cost of:	In 1991	In 2000
A medium-priced house	$248,000.00	$385,000.00
A "Whopper" at Burger King	2.35	3.75
A 4-door Honda Civic	11,800.00	18,900.00
A copy of the L.A. *Sunday Times*	1.25	2.00
A gallon of unleaded gas	1.30	2.10
A suite at the Beverly Hills Hotel	545.00	875.00
A six-pack of Michelob	4.31	7.00
A cab ride from LAX to Rodeo Drive	23.00	37.00
A first-class postage stamp	.29	.60
A round of golf at Pebble Beach	200.00	325.00
One night at Motel Six	38.00	60.00
A parking ticket in San Diego	16.00	25.00
Dinner for two at Chasen's	95.00	150.00
A hand of bananas at Safeway	1.20	2.10
One year at Stanford University	22,000.00	35,000.00
A paperback novel	5.95	9.50
A new Rolls-Royce Silver Spur	166,300.00	270,500.00
A movie	6.00	10.00

And, oh yes, a magnum of Dom Perignon, vintage 2000, will cost $315.00.

HOW LONG WILL IT TAKE TO GET TO WORK?

Commuting by the year 2000 will be a far more onerous task for many Californians, and a much easier, far less time-consuming task for others. For Californians who work in urban areas, traffic will be much worse and commuting times will be longer and more agonizing.

It is estimated that on many urban freeways, speeds will slow to less than five miles an hour during drive times. Commute times that now take thirty minutes will lengthen to an hour and more. Desperate measures will be taken to alleviate the agony of getting to work, including staggered work hours, permission to work at home when circumstances permit, and relocation of some businesses.

The exception will be for Californians who abandon the cities to work in suburbia. The trend toward finding work closer to home will be strong at the turn of the century. Millions of California workers who have marketable skills will make the difficult decision to start new careers or find new jobs just a short commute away. Distance and time spent getting to work will be a far more significant factor in accepting employment than they are today.

BY THE YEAR 2000:

Is almost certain that:

- Women will represent almost half of the total work force in California.
- Only 8.5 percent of all new workers in the state will be white males.
- Total personal income in California will exceed $1,300 billion.
- San Francisco will still have the highest per-capita personal income of any major California city.
- The average working Californian will annually earn at least $2,500 more than the average working American.
- Most Californians will take twice as long to commute to work in the city.

It is very likely that:

- The accepted retirement age will be 70 years of age.
- International marketers, management consultants, computer software operators, environmental engineers, quality control specialists, and civil service career workers will be among the professions in greatest demand.

- One out of every 6 jobs in the United States will be in California.
- The productivity of California workers will be 40 percent greater than it is today.
- The median annual household income in Marin County will exceed $100,000.

It is even possible that:

- Fewer than 2,000,000 California workers will belong to labor unions.
- Ten times the present number of FAX business messages will be sent in California every day.
- Fewer than 8 percent of California families will live at the poverty level.
- Parking for workers in the city will cost up to $25 per day.
- There will be more than 200,000 millionaires in California.

Californians on the Move

Getting into and around California has been a challenge from the earliest times. Fierce mountain ranges, searing deserts, rampaging rivers, and rugged coastlines combined to make transportation difficult from the outset. Along with one other thing: distance. California covers almost 160,000 square miles, the equivalent of Massachusetts, Vermont, Virginia, Maine, Rhode Island, New Hampshire, New York, Connecticut, and Maryland combined. A journey from the northernmost point of California to the southernmost point would also take a traveler from Washington, D.C. to Austin, Texas.

Over the decades, roadways were carved out of the wilderness, rivers were dredged for boat passage, and landing docks were built to receive sea vessels. Rail lines were extended into California and, in time, linked the northern and southern reaches of the state. With the invention of the motor car, highways were constructed between cities and towns, and new bridges were arched over rivers and bays. But somehow the burgeoning network of transportation systems never seemed quite equal to the task of moving Californians freely and openly around their state. When airplanes, airlines, and airports were added to the mix, they seemed only to multiply the problem.

Then, just before America's entry into World War II, something new came onto the scene, and Californians wondered if it might hold the answer to their hundred-year-old transportation problem. No one was quite sure what to call it, but most people sensed it would be revolutionary.

A HALF CENTURY AGO—THE FIRST FREEWAY!

On December 30, 1940, a new kind of highway was opened between Pasadena and Los Angeles. Stretching just 8.2 miles through a parklike setting, this sunken, six-lane highway was startlingly new. For a while it was referred to as the "Stopless Motorway," and then it was decided to call it "The Pasadena Freeway." Built in 33 months at a cost of $1 million-plus per mile, the freeway was expected to reduce travel time from Pasadena to Los Angeles to ten minutes, a journey that had taken the area's early settlers a full day on foot and horse.[1]

The Pasadena Freeway was designed to carry 27,000 cars daily at speeds from 45 to 70 miles an hour. It now carries 130,000 cars a day at speeds so unpredictable that the trip can take more than an hour and a half at peak drive times.[2]

The Pasadena Freeway was the forerunner of a highway system that would connect the far corners of California and give its citizens and visitors ready access to the state for the first time. The limited-access, high-speed, concrete-constructed highway was destined to dominate California transportation planning for a full half-century, carrying the state's citizenry and commerce to lengths and distances no one could foresee.

THE INTERSTATE HIGHWAY SYSTEM

The National System of Interstate and Defense Highways Act was passed by Congress in 1944 during World War II, but it wasn't until the mid-1950s that construction really got under way. With the federal government providing 90% of the funds, a network of 42,500 miles of freeways was built over the next three decades that connected almost all U.S. cities with populations of over 50,000.[3] This system will be completed well before the year 2000. It will carry more than 20 percent of all road and street traffic in the United States.

In California, the system stretches from San Diego north through Los Angeles to San Francisco and then north again into Oregon. It also runs east from San Diego and Los Angeles to Las Vegas and into northern and southern Arizona, as well as from San Francisco to Reno.

All in all, there are 2,403 miles of interstate highway in California.[4] The system in California is now essentially completed. While there will be a number of improvements and some new extensions, there will be no major additions to the system in California in this decade.

CALIFORNIA'S BUSY STREETS AND HIGHWAYS

At the present time, the entire California state highway system covers 15,025 miles with more than 47,000 lane-miles. An additional 150,000 miles of county and city roads funnel off this highway network into every corner of the state. Some 20 million licensed drivers make more than 900 million trips a day on this roadway system.[5]

If you were to place all 26 million of California's registered automobiles on the state's highways at the same time, every lane would be filled with cars bumper to bumper and every lane would be stacked three cars high![6]

Simply maintaining the state's highways now costs in excess of $600 million annually. It is estimated that annual maintenance costs alone will increase to $1.4 billion by the year 2000.[7]

Almost 150 billion miles are currently driven on California highways every year.[8] By the year 2000, this number will increase to about 260 billion miles, making California's highways the busiest in the world. The ten busiest interchanges in the United States will all be in California.

THE FUTURE OF CALIFORNIA'S HIGHWAY SYSTEM

In a few words: it's not good. Traffic congestion, the rising cost of maintenance and construction, noise, smog, and other environmental concerns all militate against the future well-being or expansion of the arterial highways of California.

For decades, freeways have been a California trademark, and the expansion of the highway system has been synonymous with California growth and development. That era is probably coming to an end.

The cost of constructing major freeways has risen enormously. In 1940, for instance, the average cost of a mile of California highway was just $1 million. In the 1990s the cost of a mile of freeway will be as much as $100 million. It is unlikely that the state will be able to build the 3,400 lane-miles and to improve the 7,700 other lane-miles which Caltrans at one time hoped to build over the next ten years. The cost would be in excess of $15 billion for construction alone![9] As Gordon Hutchins of Caltrans recently remarked, "If you want to know what our arterial highway system will look like in ten years, you can just look out the window today."[10]

The cost of maintaining the existing system is equally daunting. In the ten years between 1979 and 1989, expenditures for maintenance rose from $197 million to $587 million, a staggering increase of some 200%.

By the year 2000, state expenditures for maintenance and rehabilitation are expected to rise to $1.4 billion, far outdistancing any projection of funds available for that purpose.[11] Whether or not California will be able to protect its $100-billion-dollar investment in the state highway system is a serious question.

But even if the system is still viable in the year 2000, the prospects of traveling on it are not heartening. Whereas the state had about 11.4 million drivers and 13.1 motor vehicles in 1969, today the state has almost 19 million drivers and almost 20 million vehicles, an increase of more than 50 percent in motorists using California's surface transportation network.[12]

By the year 2000, California is expected to have 22 million drivers and 26.5 million vehicles, in addition to increased traffic from tourism. The probable effects are mind-boggling.

Authorities estimate that by the middle of the first decade of the twenty-first century, it will take fourteen additional lanes on I-80 between the Carquinez Bridge and the Bay Bridge just to maintain current rates of speed. To maintain present speeds on the Bay Bridge itself, ten additional lanes will be required. The expected average speed on Southern California's freeway system by 2010 will be 11 miles per hour, down from about 30 miles today. Some parts of the Los Angeles system of freeways may slow down to seven miles per hour by the year 2000.[13]

Traffic delays in California's central cities, suburbs, and rural areas are expected to increase from 8 to 11 percent every year between now and the end of the century, a possible increase of 110% over the past decade.

The recently passed Federal Transportation Act will give some relief to hard-pressed California transportation authorities. The act earmarked $10.5 billion dollars for California over the next six years for a variety of purposes, including highway upgrading and a variety of mass transit projects. But even these funds fall far short of what will be needed to maintain the entire state highway system.

By the year 2000, California will be saddled with a woefully inadequate highway system that will work great hardship on its citizens and continue to deteriorate well into the twenty-first century.

WHEN JUDGES SAY "NO" TO HIGHWAYS

What is probably the final nail in the coffin of any real expansion of the highway system in California was driven in December of 1990 when a U.S. District Court judge barred the construction of three major highway projects that had already been approved by other authorities.[14] This was the first time that highway building had been blocked under the Federal Clean Air Act. Stepping into a running gun battle between freeway planners and environmentalists, the judge ruled that construction cannot begin until it can be clearly demonstrated that the highways will not generate added pollution, a task which may be impossible.

Even if those particular projects do eventually receive a go-ahead, it is extremely doubtful whether more ambitious projects, such as the major widening of Interstate 90 in the East Bay and other similar expansions can ever pass the new air quality requirements. Nor is it clear that highway builders, environmentalists, and judges can agree on a new method for air pollution analysis.

IF NOT FREEWAYS—THEN WHAT?

Tollways. In 1989, the California legislature passed the Private Tollways Act (AB 680), which provided for Caltrans to request studies from private companies on the feasibility of privately owned tollways in the state. After this process was completed, a request was made for groups to submit plans for building, financing, and operating the proposed projects. To the astonishment of many policy makers, thirteen consortia submitted proposals. Companies involved included the Perot Group, First Boston Corporation, Prudential-Bache Securities, and Citicorp.[15]

Four privately financed, developed, and managed toll roads are expected to be created by the turn of the century, including completely new roadways in San Diego County, from the San Diego-Orange County line to Irvine; San Francisco East Bay; toll lanes on the Riverside Freeway; and a tolled extension on the Orange Freeway in Orange County. The total cost of these roads will be an estimated $2.5 billion.[16] This cost will be paid entirely from the private sector.

More specifically, these private tollways will probably be:
1. A 4-lane, 11.2-mile toll road extension of Route 57 in Orange County from Interstate 5 near Anaheim Stadium to Interstate 405 and connecting to State Route 72 in the vicinity of John Wayne Airport.
2. A 10-mile limited-access toll roadway (Route 125 in San Diego County) extending from State Route 905 near the Mexican border north to State Route 45; initially 4 lanes, the roadway is expected to expand later to 10 lanes including two High Occupancy Vehicle lanes.
3. A 10-mile, 4 lane/HOV road completely within the existing right-of-way on Route 91 in Orange County extending from Riverside County to State Route 55.

4. An 85-mile, 5-lane toll road from I-680 at Sunol to I-80 near Vacaville.

All four of these private toll roads will be equipped with state-of-the-art technology, allowing free-flowing traffic, even at the point of entry. Electronic monitoring devices will permit vehicles to enter at normal speeds without stopping at a toll gate. A system known as AVI (automatic vehicle identification) operates like a credit card, automatically debiting the car owner's account every time he or she enters the freeway. A toll card permitting this debit is placed in the car of every subscriber who signs up to use the system. All four of the approved toll roads plan to use this device.

Another benefit of this technology is that it permits the charge for using the highway to vary according to drive time, with higher costs being charged during periods of greatest congestion. This capacity to modulate charges is expected to "level out" use of the roadway and reduce congestion.

The toll road on the Riverside Freeway is expected to be operational by 1993 or shortly thereafter. The remaining toll roads should be on line well before the year 2000. This concept of building freeways with private funds for profit could well bring an important addition to the existing highway system in the next century. Mayor Tom Bradley of Los Angeles has already announced his own plan to seek private-sector involvement in that city's transportation system.

TRANSPORTATION IS NUMBER ONE PUBLIC CONCERN

Almost all polls of California public opinion show that Californians are more concerned about the problems of transportation than anything else in the state. In early 1991, for instance, a major regional survey in the San Francisco Bay Area showed that transportation headed the list of problems for the eighth consecutive year.[17] In fact, transportation was cited four times more frequently than any other problem, including drugs, homelessness, pollution, and crime. Of equal significance is the fact that Californians said that they were willing to accept both higher taxes and bridge tolls if those hardships would help solve the problem. They were, however, equally adamant that they were opposed to government-imposed driving restrictions and converting present highways into tolls.

Because public opinion eventually determines public policy, it can be safely concluded that the answer to California's future transportation needs will come from increases in the financial burden on the state's motorists and citizens, rather than on mandated restrictions on their travel habits.

AND IF NOT DRIVING RESTRICTIONS—THEN WHAT?

Mass transit. Californians have long been wedded to their automobiles and have regularly disdained efforts to get them to travel in the company of others in a vehicle they don't own, such as buses, trolleys, subways, trains. Californians are all too aware that mass transit takes them "from a place where they aren't starting to a place where they're not going." At the present time only 6% of all Californians regard some method of mass transit as their primary means of transportation.[18]

The propensity of Californians to travel alone in automobiles to all of their destinations will begin to change in the 1990s. As highways become more congested, as gasoline prices and the cost of automobile maintenance rise, as environmental considerations become more important, Californians will be encouraged to seek other solutions.

The bulk of California transportation funds will not be spent to construct new highways. The day of the highway builder is over. No important new public highway arterials will be built between now and the year 2000 in California. Instead, the emphasis will be on the development of new and better systems of mass transit—trains, subways, buses, and high-speed rail lines. The struggle between the motorist who wants to drive his car and the transportation planner who wants to take him out of his car will dominate all transportation issues in the 1990s.

THE POSSIBILITY OF FAST TRAINS

California transportation experts are looking carefully at high-speed trains as one possible future answer to road and air congestion. The progress of train speed has been amazing in recent decades. The French TGV high-speed train system, for instance, recently set a speed record of 320.2 miles per hour. The Paris-Lyon route has cut travel time between the two cities to less than two hours. Ultimately, it will connect Paris and London in 2 hours, 10 minutes, Paris and Frankfurt in 3 hours, and Paris and Barcelona in 4 hours, 45 minutes.[19]

European rail advocates have ambitious plans for these rapid trains. They envision them rocketing under the English Channel, through the French Alps, and across German plains. The European Transport Commission recently introduced plans for a $205 billion Western European high-speed network to be built over the next twenty years. It would include 15,500 miles of electrified track carrying trains at 200 miles an hour to all corners of the Continent.[20]

Japan is currently building a new track in the central part of the country for its ''maglev'' supertrain that will link Tokyo with Osaka in sixty minutes (instead of the present three hours) at speeds up to 300 miles an hour. The train will travel on a magnetic field ⅜ of an inch above the guideway rail.[21]

High-speed trains, however, have drawbacks. They require their own tracks because they average almost 200 m.p.h. They also require much gentler bends and are unable to follow the natural contour of the land, as do traditional trains. They also present environmental challenges and intersect existing lines and highways.

Because of these environmental considerations and the difficulty of securing clearances from California's multileveled bureaucracies, it is extremely unlikely that any trains employing this high-speed technology will be in operation in California by the turn of the century. One possible exception: Bechtel Corporation plans to build a new 300 m.p.h. train between Anaheim and Las Vegas at a cost to private investors of $5 billion.

THE POSSIBILITY OF "ALTERNATIVE-FUELED" CARS

The gasoline engine has been the standard means of motor car power in California and the nation since the beginning of the century. Environmentalists and automobile designers are now eagerly searching for an alternative to eliminate the dependence of drivers on oil and to reduce smog. Experimental solar-powered cars have been created by General Motors, Honda, the University of Michigan, and Western Washington University, among others. The World Solar Car Challenge race, held recently in Australia, featured cars from a dozen nations competing over a 1,900-mile route from Darwin to Adelaide. Averaging more than 300 miles a day and close to 40 miles per hour, these cars proved themselves worthy and reliable.[22]

Still, the most promising alternative is the electric, battery-operated car, which advocates expect to be inexpensive to operate and pollution-free. Moreover, the technology of electric cars is advancing dramatically. Several of the largest American automotive manufacturers are well along in producing practical, efficient, well-designed electric vehicles.

Chrysler Corporation has announced that by 1995 it will go into production on battery-powered minivans that will be driven by 30, 6-volt batteries, weighing 1,900 pounds, which drive an electric motor. Called the TE Vans, they will have a top speed of 65 miles per hour and travel 120 miles without recharging. It will take about nine hours to recharge the battery pack on 220-volt household current.[23]

General Motors, working with Paul MacCready, of Gossamer Condor fame, has developed a vehicle called the Impact, an experimental, battery-powered two-seater with the pickup of a sports car and a driving range that would satisfy most urban commuters. The car can travel 120 miles and be recharged in just two hours.[24] MacCready believes that with improved batteries or fuel cells, the odds are that, within a decade and a half, electric propulsion will dominate the new-car field.

The future of electric cars is bright in California. Not only is the technology available, but the need is great. California air quality officials have ordained that within the next twelve years, 200,000 such cars must be in operation on Southern California highways.

This mandate is far easier to issue than to execute, but, by the year 2000, battery-powered electric automobiles will be a common sight on the streets and highways of California.

COMING UP: SMART CARS, SMART HIGHWAYS

As automotive and highway planners become more frustrated with traffic congestion, they turn their minds and ingenuities to techno-solutions. Some solutions are now well into the planning stage and still others are already having an effect on California highways.

The Smart Corridor. A 13-mile stretch of the Santa Monica Freeway and its side streets will soon be monitored for traffic and driving conditions by computerized operations centers and the results sent to Etak Travel-pilots, electronic road maps displayed on a TV monitor on the dashboard of Oldsmobile Delta 88's built by General Motors.[25] The displays will present the driver with up to five different alternate routes to reach his destination, depending on driving conditions at the moment. Initial cost of in-car monitors will be $10,000, but mass production could bring them down to the cost of a cellular phone.

PATH. The Program for Advanced Technology of the Highway is experimenting with a system of magnets in the roadway coupled with in-vehicle sensors that will keep cars in the potentially narrower lanes of the future. Contact-avoidance systems will be designed into cars, permitting drivers on the busiest and most hazardous stretches of highway to surrender control of their vehicles to in-car and external computers working in tandem.

Automatic Braking. Radar Control Systems in San Diego is experimenting with a Collision Avoidance System. A hookup of forward radar, cruise control, and automatic braking will combine to keep the driver from plowing into the car in front, thus permitting the driver to ''tailgate safely'' on the freeway and allowing traffic to move in packs or ''platoons'' on special fast lanes.

These and other advanced schemes to solve specific traffic problems are on the drawing boards. By the year 2000, more of them will come to pass than might now be imagined. The automobile at the turn of the century will have features and conveniences that now seem unimaginable.

THE LIKELIHOOD OF GIGANTIC TRUCKS

The trucking industry is lobbying hard and effectively to have Congress enact a law to permit all states to allow bigger trucks on their highway systems. Specifically, it wants to raise the 80,000-

pound cap on truck size and let the states decide whether to allow "triple trucks" up to 120 feet long and weighing 135,000 pounds.[26]

These monster trucks, never seen on California highways, are almost ten times longer than a Honda Civic. They carry produce and matériel in a quantity that would presumably reduce transportation costs and result in lower prices. Opponents of these massive vehicles cite difficulty in driving control, particularly in windy areas, difficulty of passing for automobiles, and the threat to highway safety. The American Trucking Association, however, says that the safety record of such vehicles is excellent. Surprisingly, fourteen states, mostly in the Midwest, already permit the 120-foot-long trucks on their highways.

Because of the increased efficiency of these monster trucks in transporting goods into and through the state, look for them to be on California's highways by the year 2000.

THE POSSIBILITY OF TINY CARS

Urban planners have long dreamed of solving city traffic problems with small "urban commute cars," little gasoline-powered vehicles that might double both road and parking capacity. France is already experimenting with such microcars, and they are now seen regularly on Paris streets.

These cars are designed exclusively for in-town traffic and short commute hauls. As short as 8 feet in length, and weighing no more than 770 pounds, they can carry two passengers at the most and very little baggage, if any.[27] Their advantages are maneuverability in driving and ease of parking, as well as economy of operation. They are not as safe as larger cars, and their collision-resistance is considerably lower than that of larger cars.

The major car manufacturers in this country have no plans as of now to produce these commuter cars, but some imported vehicles of this size and type will be in evidence in California, largely on an experimental basis, by the year 2000.

CONTINUED CARNAGE ON CALIFORNIA HIGHWAYS

In the last year for which such statistics are available, Californians had a traffic accident every 56 seconds. One Californian was injured every 87 seconds. One Californian was killed every 98 seconds.[28]

This pattern has held fairly constant for a decade or so, although the safety record on California highways has improved marginally in recent years on a per-mileage-traveled basis owing to the increased use of seat belts. Nonetheless, the continuing carnage on the state's streets and highways is frightening.

In 1990, California had a total of 555,038 traffic accidents; 236,542 people were injured and 4,660 people died. In the previous five years, a total of 1,777,760 were killed or injured in California driving accidents.[29]

Looking at it another way, one out of every 5,400 persons living in California was killed in a car accident and one out of every 80 was injured. The last day on which no one died on California highways was March 11, 1968. There will be no such day between now and the year 2000.[30]

By the year 2000, present trends indicate that the number of accidents on California roadways will increase dramatically, possibly to a total of 625,000. The number of injuries will increase to 275,000. The number of deaths, however, is likely to remain relatively constant at the 5,000 level, owing to better seat belts, the increased crash-worthiness of vehicles, and the likelihood that future highway congestion will compel drivers to travel at reduced speeds.

CARS AND SMOG: THE NEW RULES

Californians have been aware of smog problems in metropolitan areas for almost half a century. After decades of regulations that control everything from smokestacks to car exhausts, and from power mowers to underarm deodorants, the air in many parts of the state is still far from clean. Now the authorities have decided that the time has come to crack down on the car driver.

Throughout the 1990s, there will be a tough, all-out fight between Californians who love to travel in their cars and state bureaucrats who are determined to pry them out from behind the wheel.

New statewide rules mandate that car makers must build automobiles that reduce exhaust pollutants by 50 to 84 percent over already stringent rules set for 1993.[31] Other regulations require the development of cleaner gasolines, as well as vehicles capable of using compressed natural gas. Auto makers must sell hundreds of thousands of "zero emission" cars in the California market in the years ahead.

Various regions in the state are coming up with their own plans of implementation. A plan for nine counties in the Bay Area is concentrating on techniques to induce commuters to abandon their automobiles for mass transit. In addition to improving rail and bus systems, the commission wants to impose higher taxes on gasoline, raise bridge tolls, and eliminate free parking at shopping malls and places of employment. Their goal is to cut automobile traffic by 35% in seven years.[32]

The effort to get Californians out of their cars and into mass transit will be largely unsuccessful. By the year 2000, personal automobiles will still be the overwhelming choice of Californians for all kinds of travel. Yet improved bus and rail systems will make minor inroads into car traffic.

Those who regard mass transit as their primary means of travel will increase from the present 6 percent to 10 or 12 percent. Smog problems will be somewhat relieved, but the goal of reducing ozone content by 25 percent below the federal standard will not be reached. The effort to cut traffic by such a dramatic amount will also fail.

DRIVER TESTING WILL GO HIGH-TECH

California is on the cutting edge of developing sophisticated methods for testing the abilities of the state's 19 million drivers. Currently, Californians who want a driver's license need only pass a brief multiple-choice test and complete a short try-out drive with an examiner.

That will certainly not be the case by the year 2000. Future applicants for a license will have to undergo a series of high-tech examinations designed to measure night and peripheral vision, glare recovery capacity, and reaction to visual cues that duplicate response time to different highway situations.

In a kind of DMV video game, the applicant will sit before a video screen that will simulate actual driving scenes. A single computerized vision test will measure such key skills as vision on darkened roadways, ability to perceive problems with peripheral vision, and speed of eye recovery from a blast of lights such as those on an approaching car. These tests will be particularly relevant to older drivers whose skills and perceptions may have declined over the years.

Licenses graded by competency will be issued by the year 2000. Some people will be permitted to drive only during the day or during nontraffic hours. Others will be licensed to drive only on certain streets and routes, or on absolutely essential trips.

THE TEMPTATION TO STAY HOME

Another solution to crowded highways that will be finding favor at the turn of the century is ''staying home.'' Communities outside California's largest cities will be increasingly occupied by a new breed of resident: the dedicated suburbanite. California's new suburbanites are dramatically changing the old relationship between the large cities and their surrounding suburbs. Unlike the previous generations of suburbanites, which almost always commuted to the cities to work and regularly to shop, many new suburbanites are staying close to home for jobs, shopping, and even entertainment.

The suburbs have grown at almost four times the rate of cities, and many suburbanites are gaining positions of both economic and political power in their own communities. Many of them no longer feel like satellites of a larger urban area, but instead look to their own smaller communities not only for their livelihood but also for their social and artistic lives. The temptation to drive into the city is slowly disappearing. Californians are refining and redefining suburbia so that they do not have to look to the larger city for most of their needs.

This new "self-contained" way of life in suburbia is in no small part a response to the difficulty of reaching the urban area. Suburbanites are staying home not just out of choice, but also in response to crowded freeways, agonizing waits at bridges and expressway entrances, and high parking fees in downtown areas.

This trend toward suburban self-reliance will continue throughout the 1990s and into the twenty-first century. Large cities will become less and less important to people who do not reside in them, and travel into the big cities by suburbanites will drop dramatically.

THE RETURN OF WALKING

With highways that are increasingly crowded, slow, and frustrating, and mass transit that is still grossly inadequate, many Californians are turning instead to the oldest of all methods of transportation: walking. Often these "commutes on foot" are up to two and three miles each way. The number of foot-commuters will continue to increase as California employers as well as transportation officials actively advocate alternate methods of commuting. Walking is also growing in popularity for other short trips such as shopping and visiting friends. "What's happening with walking is kind of like a quiet storm," says the editor of *City Sports Magazine*. "It's not like running where you have a few people at the top. This is really an activity that's worked its way into the mainstream."[33]

It is likely that, over the present decade, human locomotion will continue to grow in popularity as an alternative to street and highway travel for short- and medium-range trips.

CALIFORNIA'S CROWDED SKIES

Air traffic in California's skies is increasing dramatically every year. There are hundreds of airports throughout the state, tens of thousands of airplanes, and ten of millions of air passengers. The numbers are impressive.

TABLE 4-1
CALIFORNIA AIR STATISTICS

Public airports	260
Private airports	1,300
Heliports	600
Pilots	96,656
Commercial departures	793,056
Emplaned passengers	60,100,000
Total number of passengers in all airports	122,000,000

Source: California Department of Transportation.

Three California airports carry the bulk of California commercial traffic: Los Angeles International (37%), San Francisco (24.5%), and San Diego (9.2%).[34] Other major airports, in order, include San Jose, Ontario, John Wayne (Orange County), Oakland, Sacramento, Burbank, Long Beach, Santa Barbara, and Monterey. Traffic at all of these airports increased throughout the 1980s.

In just the past decade, airport passenger loads grew by as much as 140 percent, as in the case of the San Jose airport. San Francisco International increased by 37 percent, Oakland by 75 percent. Oakland is expected to increase by 30 percent in just this year alone.[35] Intercity travel in California is now done primarily by air, which currently accounts for almost 65% of such trips.

Surprisingly, the number of fatalities from both general aviation air traffic and commercial air traffic fell steadily through the 1980s, from 214 a year to 140.[36] This trend toward greater safety in California skies will continue into the next century despite increased air traffic.

Keeping California's skies free from gridlock is a major concern. The National Research Council estimates that the number of daily air travel passengers nationally could triple from the present 1.3 million daily to almost 4 million by the year 2040.

Preventing gridlock in the next century could require as many as ten major new airports, thousand-seat jets, and hundreds of billions of dollars. Those efforts, however, will not take place in this decade but will, instead, remain in the planning stage. Four

new less-ambitious public airports will be established in California, however, by the year 2000: Hamilton, Norton, Mather, and George.

A "TRANSPORTATION CAMPUS" FOR CALIFORNIA

It is possible that before the next century, California will be the home of a vast research "theme park" or campus devoted to the development of transportation technology. Already in the planning stages, it is receiving support from business, government, and academia. Advance proposals call for a 2,000-acre campus, which the state legislature has mandated be located somewhere in the Sacramento area. The facility would include special laboratories for research and development of advanced highway, rail, and aviation systems. Specialized engineers and scientists would work in ultramodern facilities that include nine miles of freeway, eight interchanges, and six miles of arterial roads and city streets. Under development would be magnetic-levitation trains, levitated pedestrian "people movers," fuel-efficient "smart automobiles," and intelligent highways that automatically convey vehicles to their destination.

More than $1 billion in private and public start-up money will be spent on this transportation complex over the next decade. Tentatively named "The Western National Research and Development Center," it will be one of the most ambitious projects of its type ever undertaken, and its goal will be to restore California to its lost superiority in transportation technology. The town of Sutter Bay is currently front-running as the site for this extraordinary project, and ground could be broken as early as 1995.

BY THE YEAR 2000:

It is almost certain that:

• Traffic on some California freeways will slow to an average of about ten miles an hour.

- The new Boeing 777, holding up to 400 passengers and featuring folding wings, will be landing at California's major airports.
- More than 5,000 people will be killed annually on California's highways.
- More than 30 million vehicles will be registered in California, along with more than 24 million drivers.
- Toll roads will begin to play a prominent role in the state's transportation mix.
- All of the Bay Area's earthquake-damaged highway structures will be replaced by new, improved surface freeways, including the Embarcadero and the Cypress.
- The number of passengers using California's 43 air-carrier airports will rise by at least 50%.
- The interstate highway system, commenced in California in 1956, will finally be completed.
- San Franciscans will be able to take BART directly to San Francisco International Airport.
- A new 17.4-mile metro rail subway system built at a cost of more than half a billion dollars will link Los Angeles and North Hollywood.
- Caltrain will extend its line directly into downtown San Francisco.
- Ice and weather sensors placed in freeways will inform authorities by computer which highway areas have weather problems, where freezing is occurring, where snow is accumulating, where sand, salt, or plowing is required to keep highways open.
- Commuters and tourists will be able to buy a "California Pass," similar to the present Eurailpass, that will be usable for all federal, state, and municipal trains in the state.
- The number of HOV lanes in California will more than double.
- Speed limits on California freeways will be unchanged.
- More than 35 percent of all California drivers will have no automobile insurance.

It is very likely that:

- More than $100 million, three times what the bridge originally cost, will be spent on the Golden Gate Bridge to make it more earthquake-proof.

- State expenditures on mass transit systems will reach $2 billion annually.
- Los Angeles County will have the nation's second-largest transit system, its largest car-pool lane network, and its biggest bus fleet.
- San Francisco's International Airport will have an entirely new passenger terminal, built at a cost of $1.4 billion.
- All persons seeking a license to drive a motorcycle will have to complete a special safety training course.
- A completely new rail system will link San Jose, Oakland, and Sacramento, with three-trip-a-day service carrying up to 12,550 passengers daily between the three cities.
- Huge three-trailer trucks will travel California's highways.
- A new ground-level metro rail will run from Universal City to North Hollywood.
- There will be more than 100,000 battery-powered electric automobiles on California highways.

It is even possible that:

- Californians will be able to travel from Anaheim to Las Vegas by high-speed train in 75 minutes.
- A motorist stopped for a traffic violation will be able to pay his fine on the spot with a credit card that will be processed by the traffic officer in his patrol car.
- All of California's major bridges, including the Golden Gate, the Bay, the San Diego-Coronado, will offer bar-coded window stickers that will permit patrons to drive through specified toll lanes and be charged without stopping.
- A sleek new, 70-miles-per-hour commuter train will link downtown Los Angeles with Simi Valley, San Bernardino, and the Newhall-Saugus area.
- A new bridge will span the southern portion of San Francisco Bay.
- A huge new international airport will straddle the border between the United States and Mexico at San Diego.

5

The Educated Californians

Nothing will be more important in determining the long-range future of California than the state's ability to educate its young people. The increasingly sophisticated and demanding jobs of the future will require employees who are well-grounded in all the basic intellectual skills, as well as those who are specially trained in the sciences and humanities. Yet there is a real question as to whether or not the educational system of California is prepared to provide what will be required.

Californians have come to realize that the quality of education affects everyone in the state, regardless of age or race. A recent poll ranked education as the most important policy issue in California.[1] At the same time, Californians gave their local schools a low "C" grade in performance. Small wonder: California youngsters, compared with those of other states, are on the average less likely to study the sciences, less likely to graduate from high school, and less likely to go to college.

Fewer than seven out of ten students in California who start the third grade actually complete their high school education. California's student-teacher ratio is the worst in the nation.[2]

The shortcomings of the state's public schools can be seen in these two facts: in the third grade, the state's pupils rank slightly ahead of the national average in reading and writing, and they are way ahead in math. By the twelfth grade, they rank well below national norms in reading and writing and slightly below in math.[3]

On the other hand, there are some bright spots in the California educational picture. The state ranks fourth in the nation in SAT scores (only New Hampshire, Oregon, and Vermont do better).[4] The state's university system is one of the most comprehensive in the country, and the University of California is so popular with students both in and out of state that the system has been forced to plan significant expansion.

Moreover, Californians have now become seriously concerned about improving their educational institutions, especially at the K-12 level. There is every reason to believe that the years between now and the millennium will see a concerted effort at all levels to bring California education up to an improved level.

Look for significant attention, in terms of both policy focus and revenue allocation, to be brought to bear on education in California by politicians, legislators, educators, parents, students, business, and the public between now and the year 2000.

"BABY BOOM ECHO" WILL GLUT THE SCHOOLS

Virtually unheralded, the so-called baby-boomers born in the decade following World War II have created a large next-generation of youngsters about to enter the school system of California. The children of this "baby boom echo" constitute a veritable tidal wave of preschoolers poised to sweep into the state's schools. Most of the schools are ill-prepared to receive them.

In San Francisco, for instance, 35,000 children are expected to hit the public schools during the next five years. The Richmond school district has 12,155 children under 5 years of age, far more than those now in the first five grades. Oakland has 14 percent more preschoolers than it does children 5 to 9 years of age.[5] To complicate the educational task, according to a statewide survey among children who will reach school age in the next four years, a majority are minorities. More than 35 percent are Hispanic, 9 percent are black, and 10 percent are Asian.[6]

The major reason for this bottleneck of too-many-youngsters heading for too-few-schoolrooms is the unforeseen increase in the birthrate during the past five years. The "baby boomers" are simply far more prolific than many educators had anticipated. The census

FIGURE 5-1
GROWTH IN CALIFORNIA SCHOOL-AGE POPULATION,
1990–2000

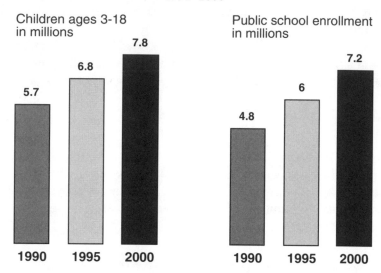

Source: California Department of Education and U.S. Census Bureau

demonstrates clearly that birthrates have risen to levels not seen since the early 1960s.

The 1990s will see an extraordinary number of students entering the public school system, and this "bubble" on the demographic charts will continue to the year 2000. The already strained resources of the elementary school system, and later the high school system, will be stretched to the breaking point during the decade.

HOW MANY STUDENTS?

The population of California will swell to at least 35 million by the end of the decade, with an additional 5 million people living and working in the state. Many of these new California immigrants will be young families with children who will enter the California educational system. When their numbers are added to the state's present 4.8 million public school students, the total school population will swell dramatically. The number of school-age children and the number of public school students in the state are already forecast through the end of the century.

These numbers represent 1,200,000 additional students by the middle of the decade, and the odds are overwhelming that those numbers will continue to mount well into the next century. The total public school population in California will exceed 7 million by the year 2000. Never before in history has any state attempted to provide educational facilities and adequate schooling for such a staggering number of young people.

THE CHANGING ETHNICITY OF THE STATE'S STUDENT POPULATION

Just as the overall population of California will undergo dramatic changes in its ethnic makeup by the year 2000, so, too, will the ethnic character of the California public school population change.

FIGURE 5-2
CALIFORNIA SCHOOL POPULATION BY RACE, 1990

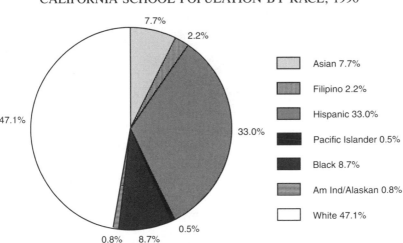

Source: California Department of Education.

A little more than two decades ago, the average California school-room was predominantly white. Three out of every four California students belonged to the white majority. The only significant minorities were Hispanic, with less than 14 percent, and black, with little more than 8 percent. Just twenty years later, those numbers are dramatically changed. White students are now a minority, and Hispanics represent a full third of the student body. By the year 2000, the student population will undergo yet another dramatic transformation.

As the state public school system enters the twenty-first century, the highest percentage of students in K-12 will be Hispanic, occupying roughly the same percentage that white students do today. White students, on the other hand, will be approximately the one-third that Hispanics represent today. Blacks will remain at about the same percentage that they do now. The percentage of Asians, however, will have almost doubled.

The changing character of the California student population will affect state public education in many ways, including language requirements, curriculum demands, and teacher qualifications.

HOW MANY NEW CLASSROOMS?

With the school population reaching 7 million by the year 2000, the state will have to embark on a major school construction program. All in all, California schools will have an average of 220,000 additional students every year, or well over 2 million additional by the end of the decade.[8] If schools average thirty students per classroom (slightly greater than the present average), the state will need more than 70,000 new classrooms by the year 2000.

For all practical purposes, California will need one new elementary school every Monday morning for the rest of this decade. Even then, the prospects of curing the overcrowding are not good.

If an average of nineteen new classrooms is built in California every day, including weekends and holidays, between now and

the year 2000, at the end of that time classrooms will be just as crowded as they are now.

WHO WILL PAY—AND HOW?

Funding California education in the 1990s will be a staggering responsibility, a task without parallel in U.S. history. The average cost of educating a pupil in the state's public schools is $4,279.00 a year. Total annual revenues required for operations at present are close to $20 billion.[9] The cost of building the new schoolrooms required by the year 2000 could be about $30 billion by itself. The main funding sources, as in the past, will be local taxes, state legislative appropriations, federal assistance, bond issues, and, of course, the California State Lottery.

It is unlikely, however, that the lottery can be counted on to provide any large share of the needed future funds. Contrary to popular notion, the lottery has not proved to be the salvation of California education. Lottery sales have reached about $2.6 billion and have provided about $1 billion for public education. Allocation of these funds to kindergarten through grade 12 schools has been about $805 million, or less than $170 per student.[10] It is not likely that these funds or allocations will experience any significant increase in the decade ahead.

The question, then, is where the funding will come from to build all the schools and classrooms necessary to house and teach such a staggering school population. Since November 1988, California voters have approved $3.2 billion in school construction bonds, but the recent history of bond approvals is discouraging. Voter approvals have been dropping with each election—from 65 percent in June 1988 to 61 percent in November 1988, to 57.5 percent in June 1990.[11]

Bond issues for schools now require a two-thirds vote of the electorate, a major hurdle in achieving voter approval. This system will change by the year 2000. A constitutional amendment will be in place by that time that will lower the needed approval to a simple majority of those voting. This change will

help make it possible to fund the construction needed to educate California's school-age youngsters.

TEACHERS: IF THEY'RE GOOD, THEY'RE WORTH IT

The latest annual report by the National Education Association shows that the average public school teacher in California makes nearly $40,000 a year. Only four states pay their teachers more; thirty-seven states pay less. In the past year, the average California teacher received a 4.2 percent raise. The average pay for a public school teacher in the U.S. is $33,015, or about $6,500 less than his or her California counterpart. [12]

Another way of looking at teacher cost is what the state pays per pupil. The U.S. average is $2,422. The California teacher cost-per-pupil is only slightly higher at $2,654. [13]

By the year 2000, the average teacher in California's public schools will be paid almost $50,000 a year, and the cost-per-pupil in the state will be more than $7,100. Both figures will be at the top or near the top of the national rankings.

THE GROWING PROBLEM OF LANGUAGE

All the problems confronting California education seem magnified by the fact of extreme multilingualism. With the overwhelming number of immigrants coming to the state, the schools must constantly deal with a high percentage of students who speak other languages. Every year, more than 100,000 children who speak little or no English enter the California school system.

In the Los Angeles school district, for instance, English and Spanish are the most commonly spoken languages, but other languages used are Korean, Cantonese, Armenian, Vietnamese, Filipino, Farsi, and Cambodian. The argument over whether all these children need to be taught in their native languages will continue throughout the 1990s. Advocates of multiple-language education will argue that teaching school children in their family languages preserves their ethnic identity and advances the concept of a multicultural society. Others will continue to argue that bilingual education is a failure, that it is unnecessarily expensive, and that it does not prepare students to compete in the real world.

The basic premise of bilingual education, of course, is that it will make minority children equally literate in two languages. The burden on the school system, however, will grow greatly in the years ahead as immigration increases and the babble of languages in California continues to multiply. In the twenty-two years since bilingual education began, the number of different languages represented in the schoolrooms nationally has grown to 153.[15] The cost and complexity of instructing school children in their native languages, as well as in English, will force a rethinking of the practicality of extensive bilingual education.

By the year 2000, bilingual education will still be a significant part of the California curriculum, but the trend will be toward English-intensive instruction. The segregative and costly aspects of multiple-language teaching will be more and more replaced with a fuller and more effective education in English, which is the empowering language of our national and state societies.

AN ACTIVE ROLE FOR CALIFORNIA BUSINESS

Businessmen in California are seriously concerned about the educational level of the present and future California work force. Realizing that well-educated and highly skilled manpower is essential to its well-being, California business will take a more active role in the state education system in the decade ahead. Its present concern is expressed by the California Business Roundtable, which recently asked its members to rank the need for ten potential state policies. More than 80 percent supported a comprehensive reform of the state's education system. One member reported that 60 percent of the company's job applicants cannot pass an examination geared for a seventh-grade education. A number of California businesses have had to establish their own remedial reading classes in order to assure themselves of a sufficient work force for their own needs. Sam Ginn, chairman of Pacific Telesis, says, "We need workers with skills that will allow us to be competitive into the next century. These aren't skills we're getting out of the public education system."[16]

The agenda that California business will be advocating for California schools includes additional emphasis on student achievement, frequent testing against statewide standards, more parental involvement, merit pay for teachers, and giving parents the right to select which school their children will attend.

Look for California business generally, as well as individual business executives, to become actively involved in bringing about change in the California public education system in the 1990s.

"SURVIVAL OF THE FITTEST" SCHOOLS

Education reform groups in California and elsewhere are strongly advocating "school choice," that is, giving parents the right to select the school to which they send their children, rather than being told which school they must attend. Supporters of the concept claim that by enabling parents to choose among public schools—or even to send their offspring to private schools through the use of vouchers—they will unleash "market forces" that will reward the good schools, shake out the bad ones, and force the inadequate schools to improve. Opponents claim there is no empirical evidence that such a system will work, and they also question the use of public funds to send children to private schools.

This idea of "survival of the fittest" schools has been used with some success in other areas of the country. Cambridge, Massachusetts, a city of 98,000, installed the system in 1989, and it has already forced the weaker, less well-run schools to improve in order to survive. After one of the least effective Cambridge schools saw its enrollment fall by over half, it installed a completely new curriculum, upgraded teachers, and hired a new principal.[17] Advocates of the "choice" system point to the Cambridge results as a clear indication that the technique bodes well for the future.

Between now and the year 2000, "school choice" experiments will be conducted in a number of school districts in California, despite opposition from the state's education establishment. The results will be generally positive with an overall upgrading in the

quality of the schools and an increase in student test scores for the districts involved.

SCHOOLS FOR PROFIT?

A private corporation, Whittle Communications, has announced plans to create a network of 200 schools nationwide.[18] The schools would be operated for profit and make heavy use of innovative teaching techniques. The first phase of the system will be the establishment of a laboratory school in Knoxville, Tennessee, where educators, scientists, and political leaders will spend the next two years establishing a curriculum, devising teaching methods, and designing a model school. Duplicate schools will then be established in all fifty states, with a number of them in California.

Students will be selected randomly from a pool of students, with 20 percent of them receiving scholarships, except in areas where there is a system of free choice among schools. In the early years, the corporation expects to make a profit from tuition, but after that the corporation would make its money by selling the educational software it develops to public schools.

The Deputy Secretary of Education, Ted Sanders, describes the Whittle experiment as "the kind of break-the-mold schools called for in the president's education strategy." The plan, of course, has its detractors. Albert Shanker, president of the American Federation of Teachers, says: "To the extent to which large numbers of learning youngsters are pulled out of public schools, there is a possibility that the public schools could begin to look like the charity wards of hospitals."[19]

Nevertheless, there is a good chance that this and other private for-profit school experiments will be under way soon in California and other parts of the nation. By the year 2000, the concept of privately operated schools run for profit will be well accepted in California, with a number of successful and respected elementary institutions functioning in the central and southern parts of the state.

CATHOLIC SCHOOLS WILL MAKE A COMEBACK

Catholic schools in California, long a mainstay of the state's educational mix, have been in decline for the past several decades.

Nationwide, Catholic high schools are closing at an average of twenty-five per year, and elementary schools are closing at four times that rate. The principal reason is that Catholic schools have not followed their constituency to the suburbs.

Over the past years, the exodus to the suburbs has created a separation of Catholic students from Catholic schools in California. In San Francisco, for instance, five of the twelve Catholic high schools that were open five years ago are now closed. In the eighteen burgeoning cities of Contra Costa County, there are only three high schools to serve Catholic students. Cost, of course, is also a factor. A Catholic high school education in California costs a student $2,500 a year.[20]

Catholic educators are now planning a renaissance for their schools. It will have two basic tenets. The first is to build more schools in the suburbs, where their natural constituency seems to be migrating. A ten-year program of suburban school construction is now under way. The second will be a serious and intensive marketing campaign to attract students of all faiths and backgrounds. Non-Catholics already constitute more than 20 percent of all Catholic school students, and a sophisticated program will be undertaken to enlarge this number significantly in the years ahead.

By the year 2000, the erosion of Catholic schools in California, at both the elementary and high school level, will have ceased. Catholic schools will again be attracting significant numbers of students and will be educating a higher percentage of the overall student population than they are at the present time.

CALIFORNIA AND NATIONAL TESTING

California has long honored the tradition of state and local autonomy in its public education system. Now the Secretary of Education has called for a system of national examinations in the elementary and secondary schools. Under the proposal, all of the nation's children, including those in California, would be measured against a single standard in five academic subjects—history, geography, math, science, and English—during the fourth, eighth, and twelfth grades. These tests, it is argued, would raise academic standards across the nation and give students, parents, teachers, and academics a clear measurement of how their own schools are doing. There must be something in favor of such national tests: the United States is the only industrialized nation that does not test all of its students for mastery of academics.[21]

California critics of the national testing plan charge, among other things, that it would lead inevitably to a national curriculum, and ultimately to the homogenizing of intellectual life. Advocates, on the other hand, advance the idea that such tests would bring badly needed coherence to studies in California schools, while leaving local educators their choice of teaching methods and materials. Advocates also stress that national testing would be optional, not mandatory. The latter point, however, may be moot, since college admissions officers and prospective employers would no doubt insist on seeing national test scores for individuals. Students not taking the tests would stand a good chance of being left out of the selection process.

The argument will rage on through most of the 1990s in California and throughout the nation. Increasingly, however, leaders in labor, business, politics, and education will come to the conclusion that national testing is one sure way to pressure local educators to raise academic standards and to concentrate on developing the skills that students need to compete effectively in later life.

Top California school administrators at the state level will strongly resist the imposition of "American Achievement Tests" on California public school students as an intrusion on local authority. But national testing is a concept whose time has come. By the year 2000, California students will be taking tests every four years to see how they stack up against the national norm.

YEAR-ROUND EDUCATION IN CALIFORNIA

The great majority of public schools in California are in operation for only two-thirds of the calendar year, then closed for the three months of summer. Within the next ten years, this schedule of operation will change dramatically. By the year 2000, the majority of California schools will function on a year-round basis.

The trend is already clear. By mid-1990, in more than 600 schools throughout the state, 11 percent of the state's public school students K-12 were in year-round attendance. The number of school districts changing to a full-year schedule increased 42 percent over the previous year, a growth factor that will continue through the decade.[22] The reasons for this trend are obvious. First, districts are seeking relief from school overcrowding resulting from their inability to match student growth with school construction. Secondly, the original system, based on an agricultural economy in which children's presence at home was essential in the summer, is no longer valid in a modern, industrial economy.

Year-round school operation in California takes two directions. In one instance, the 180 days are spread throughout the year. Typically, students and their teachers are present in school at the same time periods of sixty days of instruction and twenty days of vacation, repeated three times a year. The second type of year-round education is called "multitracking." This system employs three to five "tracks" of students, rotating their use of the school and its facilities throughout the year. If, for instance, a school uses a four-track system, then at any one time, three of the tracks are using the school while the fourth is on vacation. When the fourth track returns to school, another track starts its vacation period. Thus, the entire student population rotates in and out of school throughout the year. The principal advantage of "multitracking" is a more efficient use of the school facilities, but it also allows for new opportunities in teacher training and reduces student burnout, which sometimes occurs during a long period of unrelieved study.

The trend toward year-round education in California's schools will continue throughout the 1990s. By the millennium, almost half of all California public school students will be attending year-round schools.

WHY NOT LENGTHEN THE SCHOOL YEAR?

California, and the United States in general, has one of the shortest school years in the civilized world. On the average, California students spend the equivalent of only six months worth of

TABLE 5-1

NUMBER OF DAYS SPENT IN SCHOOL DURING THE YEAR

United States	180
Sweden	180
Scotland	200
Israel	215
South Korea	220
Japan	243

Source: Good Housekeeping, October 1990.

days in the classroom. Most industrialized nations require children to spend more time on their schooling, and a number of nations have a considerably longer school year.

There are good arguments for extending the school year in California, the most important of which is the need to make the state's students more competitive in their scholastic achievements.

However, school budget restrictions, combined with protective teacher unions, make it extremely unlikely that there will be any serious consideration of lengthening the time that California students spend in the classroom. In the year 2000, California youngsters will still be going to school an average of only 180 days out of the year.

WHY SCHOOLS CAN'T DO IT ALL

The average Californian, between birth and 18 years of age spends only 9 percent of his or her time in school. The other 91 percent is spent under the jurisdiction of other environments, primarily the family home.[23]

This percentage could conceivably increase to 10 percent by the year 2000 because of the increased emphasis on education, but 90 percent of the average child's time until he reaches adulthood will still be spent outside the influence of the schoolroom.

THE SURGE IN HIGHER EDUCATION

Enrollment in California's colleges and universities has been growing steadily ever since the state system was established. At the present time, almost two million graduate and undergraduate students are enrolled in the University of California, the California state universities, and the California community colleges. The University of California has more than 160,000 students at its nine locations in the state.

By the year 2000, the university will enlarge its capacity by adding at least three new locations. The first of these will be built in the Central Valley, probably in Porterville in Tulare County. This campus will cost $300 million to build and $100,000 a year to operate. Within twenty years, Porterville will have a population of 100,000 people. Later, the second new campus will be built in Northern California and a third in the southern part of the state.

Despite the growing population of California and the increasing number of high school graduates (by the year 2000, 275,000 students will be graduating every year), the University of California will slowly shrink its student population over the next three to four years. Because of budget restrictions imposed by the legislature, the university will become smaller in terms of number of students before it expands later in the decade by building new campuses. The tool for making this reduction will be higher standards in terms of grade average and in SAT scores.

Future grade-average requirements will increase from 3.1 to 3.3, and SAT scores for math and English required for admission will be 1300 instead of 1100. Annual registration fees will also be increased to $2,500. These changes are expected to reduce enrollment by at least 5,500 students within the next several years.

In the long run, however, pressure on the university system to broaden its constituency, plus the growing population of candidates for admittance, will force the university to increase its acceptance total, and the total campus population will grow by at least 10,000 by the end of the decade.

The community college system embraces 72 different campuses servicing almost 1,500,000 students.[25] Pressure on these facilities to expand will also be tremendous over the next ten years.

It is likely that as many as ten new campuses will be added to the community college system by the year 2000, and the total student enrollment will swell by an additional 200,000 students. By the year 2000, the total enrollment of all California institutions of higher learning will exceed 2.3 million students.

BY THE YEAR 2000:

It is almost certain that:

- The student enrollment in California's public school system will exceed 7 million.
- California will have built an average of twenty new classrooms every day for the past ten years.
- The state will be spending over $200 million a year just for textbooks.
- California will have some 65,000 foreign students, almost 20 percent of the U.S. total.
- The University of California will have three new campuses.
- Minority students will constitute almost 50 percent of the student body in all K-12 California schools.
- Less than 7 percent of California school children will be in private schools.
- Undergraduate tuition at Stanford University will be more than $20,000 a year, and the average undergraduate's annual cost to attend Stanford will be $35,000.
- More than 20 percent of all student loans in California will be in default.
- California will still have more than thirty one-room schoolhouses.

It is very likely that:

- California will still rank last in the U.S. in teacher-pupil ratios.
- More women than men will earn university doctorates in California.
- More than 95 percent of all private schools in California will be coeducational.

- The University of California will have more than 180,000 students enrolled on all its campuses.
- The state's public school teachers, now 82 percent white, will be only 65 percent white.
- The California State Lottery will contribute less than 2 percent of the overall state public school budget.
- The average elementary school teacher in California will be paid more than $50,000 a year.
- Crime in the California public schools—mostly theft, arson, and vandalism—will cost the state almost $40 million annually.
- One out of every five adults in California will be functionally illiterate in the English language.
- Educating a child for four years at a state-supported college will cost more than $75,000.

It is even possible that:

- The law will require that children in California start school at the age of 4.
- Less than 10 percent of the total enrollment in the Los Angeles public school system will be white.
- More than 100,000 violent crimes will be committed in a year in the state's public schools.
- Sending a child to a private university in California for four years will cost almost $150,000.
- Most California children will go to year-round schools.

6

The California Breadbasket

California's agriculture, a complex of produce growers, livestock raisers, small farmers, and giant agribusinesses, constitutes an $18 billion conglomerate industry. But even that awesome number fails to communicate its true impact on the state or its importance to Californians. A large percentage of the state's freight traffic is involved in the transportation of farm produce from one point to another. California helps support a giant chemical industry by using more than 30 percent of all the pesticides in the country.[1] A large amount of the gas and oil produced in California is used by the state's agriculture. Agriculture uses more than 80 percent of all the water in California. The industry employs hundreds of thousands of people in the course of a single year. Just over 32 percent of California land is farmland.[2]

The importance of California agriculture to the nation as a whole is equally impressive. California is a runaway first among all 50 states in cash farm receipts, trouncing second-place Texas by a whopping 65 percent.[3] California produces more than half of all the fresh vegetables in the United States. California is the country's largest producer of a whole host of major food commodities, and the exclusive producer of many others. Of the top ten agricultural counties in the United States, eight are in California. California agriculture historically grows at a rate that exceeds the national average.[4]

This year, total receipts will exceed $19 billion in gross income. By the year 2000, California agriculture will be an even more dominant industry, with revenues approaching $30 billion.

CALIFORNIA HELPS FEED THE NATION

The American diet would be dramatically altered without the munificence of California's agriculture. From almonds to walnuts, California is the major producer of many of America's favorite foods.

A look at California's dominance in the U.S. market in various produce categories gives a clear picture of the state's role in feeding America.

In all, California accounts for most of U.S. production of 58 different crop and livestock commodities. A number of crops, including almonds, artichokes, dates, figs, kiwis, olives, nectarines, pistachios, pomegranates, prunes, raisins, and walnuts, are grown nowhere else in America. California in a very real sense feeds most of America, and a good part of the world as well. It is almost

TABLE 6-1

CALIFORNIA AS PRIMARY PRODUCER OF FOOD CROPS

Commodity	U.S. Rank	% of U.S. Production
Almonds	1	100
Avocados	1	91.8
Broccoli	1	90
Carrots	1	50
Cauliflower	1	75
Celery	1	71.3
Dried Prunes	1	100
Strawberries	1	74
Tangerines	1	52.7
Figs	1	100
Grapes	1	88.5
Lemons	1	67.9
Lettuce	1	67.9
Honeydew Melons	1	77
Nectarines	1	100
Olives	1	100
Onions	1	29.4
Peaches	1	60.5
Pears	1	38.7
Pistachios	1	100
Plums	1	82.1
Pomegranates	1	100
Walnuts	1	100

Source: California Department of Food and Agriculture.

impossible to exaggerate the importance of California's agriculture to the well-being of the state and the nation.

By the year 2000, America's dependence on California agriculture will be even greater as the population of the country continues its westward movement and as California farmers become even more productive.

WILL CALIFORNIA AGRICULTURE DIE OF THIRST? THE BIG BATTLE FOR WATER IN THE 1990s

Agriculture in the state now faces one of the most daunting challenges in its history: the preservation of its vital water supply. Until 1990, the fourth year of the current drought, water allocations to agriculture were generally considered sacred, and few questions were asked as the state's farmers, year after year, used more than 80 percent of all the allocable water in California. But with California reservoirs drying up and urban areas facing punitive restrictions in the early months of 1991, California farmers faced the first significant threat to their access to the state's water in over half a century.

In early 1991, the State Department of Water Resources announced that it would stop immediately all deliveries of water from the State Water Project to California farms. Federal water projects also made significant cuts to farmers. The result is that water available for agriculture will drop about 20 percent, a staggering decline in the agricultural water supply. It is estimated that, as a result of water shortages, 600,000 acres of agricultural land, 6 percent of the state's farmland, lay fallow in 1991.[4]

In the future, farmers will be more and more dependent on groundwater pumped from wells. But the years of drought have seriously sapped the state's supply of groundwater as well, and it is now in seriously short supply. Almost all farmers must now dig deeper and at greater expense, and the water they find is not always the best. In the Alta Irrigation District near Fresno, for instance, farmers are starting to pump up seawater.

There is a demonstrable relationship between water availability and agricultural revenues. It is estimated that state farmers had about 20 percent less water in 1991 with which to grow their crops. Revenues were expected to drop about 10 percent, the first decline in many years. If it were not for increased prices due to commodity shortages, the decline would be even greater.

Lack of water in a single year can also cause damage that is long lasting. Fruit and nut trees deprived of water for a single season can be lost forever. The same is true of vines. In Kern County, for instance, more than 20,000 acres planted with permanent crops such as almonds, pistachios, and other fruit trees, have no water except that provided by the State Water Project. If the trees can get enough water to stay alive, the county will sustain an estimated loss of only $395 million in direct crop loss. But if the trees cannot be irrigated enough to be kept alive, then the loss will rise to $8.4 billion in permanent tree damage.[5]

The 600,000 acres of California farmland idled in 1991 as a result of the drought represent about 6 percent of the state's total farmland. The total loss in production and revenue is estimated to have been in excess of $1 billion. Even the so-called "March Miracle" of unanticipated rainfall in 1991 did not have much effect on those sad numbers. As the manager of one major farming water district says, "I don't think the numbers will change much because of these last rains. . . . We're telling our growers not to anticipate any additional water supplies."[6]

Droughts can be especially hard on California dairy farmers. When dairy farmers are deprived of their normal water sources, they have no alternative but to truck water in for their herds. The water itself is expensive enough, but trucking expenses can be almost prohibitive. A farmer with 600 head must haul in as much as 14,000 gallons a day at a cost of up to $12,000 a month.[7] The cost of hay, a water-intensive crop, is also dramatically increased during a drought, bringing still another financial burden to dairy farmers.

Water shortages, and the fear of future droughts, will, of course, affect farmers in different ways, depending on the commodity involved.

Rice: The most water-intensive of all California crops, rice literally grows in water. By the year 2000, many rice farmers will have converted to other crops or sold their land for other uses.

Cotton: One of California's leading crops, cotton and cotton seed represent almost 6 percent of the state's agricultural economy. In 1991, water shortages reduced production dramatically, generating a loss of a billion dollars under normal revenues. In the year 2000, cotton will be a less important factor in California's agricultural picture, with some cotton fields converted to crops that demand less water.

Artichokes: Grown largely with water from deep wells, the artichoke crop will not be affected by a shortage of surface water. Lower water tables, however, could affect production negatively if droughts continue.

Beef: The drought has already wiped out thousands of acres of range land where cattle graze. As a result, the cattle count in California has been seriously reduced. In some counties, cattle numbers have shrunk by up to 50 percent since 1986. By the year 2000, beef production will be dramatically reduced in California. Even if there is sufficient water for grazing lands, the fear of future droughts will be sufficient to keep cattle raisers from enlarging their herds to any great extent.

Grapes: Growers of wine grapes who irrigate their vineyards from aquifers are having drought difficulties. Many have cut back on production, and some are sacrificing current harvests to save their vines for future years. Table grape growers who have switched to water-efficient drip irrigation systems are weathering the drought with little difficulty. By the year 2000, the entire grape/wine industry will have switched to drip irrigation methods and will have little to fear from future droughts.

Hay: Alfalfa is a water-intensive crop, and production generally suffers during drought. By the end of the century, alfalfa production in California will decrease because of reduced demand, and growers will tend to concentrate in areas such as Kern County, where groundwater wells offer protection against the dangers of drought.

Dairy: The dairy industry will remain healthy in California, despite any water shortages, because of strong demand at the consumer level. However, by the year 2000, prices of most dairy products in the state will have increased considerably because grazing land has been reduced and because of the increased cost of hay resulting from decreased alfalfa production.

The principal impact of California's recent drought on agriculture, however, will be that it has called into question the inherent right of the state's farmers to monopolize the water supply. Historically,

California farmers have had friends in the right places and in the right political offices. But the politics of water shortages have brought about the first real challenge to agriculture's "divine right" to 80 percent of the state's water supply. Says Lance Barnett, economist at the State Department of Commerce, "The state's water supply has to be reallocated, essentially away from agriculture, because that's where the water is now, to urban and business uses."[8]

By the year 2000, California agriculture's dominant use of the state's water supply will continue, but it will diminish from 80 percent to about 70 percent. The effect of this reduction will be a major shift away from water-intensive crops such as rice, alfalfa, cotton, and cattle. The state's farmers will make a determined effort to reduce their reliance on more restrictive water allocations by converting to deep water wells and by developing new methods of drip irrigation to conserve water supplies.

Overall, California agriculture's leadership position in America will not be seriously affected by the drought. It will adapt, invent, refine, and shift, but it will remain the provider of more than half of the nation's fruits, nuts, and vegetables.

THE BIG FREEZE OF 1990: A LASTING LEGACY

With most of the media attention concentrated on the recent drought, many Californians not directly involved in agriculture have not sufficiently appreciated the second great devastation to the state's farms: the big freeze of 1990. Just before Christmas of that year, temperatures plummeted to the low 20s and high teens in most farming areas of California. It was a freeze that caught most farmers unprepared and wreaked almost unimaginable damage on crops and trees.

In total, it is estimated that the December freeze of 1990 caused over $700 million in damage to California agriculture. And, as a result, some 15,000 farm workers and packers were laid off their jobs.[9]

Less publicized was the fact that the primary source of new citrus trees to replace those killed by the freeze was also severely damaged. Known as the foundation block, it is a six-acre stand of lemon, lime, grapefruit, orange, and citrus trees surrounded by a chain-link fence and barbed wire at the University of California Lindcove Field Station in Tulare County. Normally, budwood is sliced from these specially grown, protected, and disease-free trees and used to replant and replenish California orchards. Set up to protect California's $1 billion citrus industry, Lindcove ordinarily sells 70,000 buds a year. But the freeze damaged the buds on almost all of the station's 400 valuable trees.[10] As a result, Lindcove Field, the only source of buds tested and cleared of viruses, was unable to sell any buds for the eighteen months following the freeze. The result is that most California orchards damaged by the great freeze had to delay their programs to replenish and reestablish for more than a year.

The impact of the long-term damage to California's nut and citrus industry resulting from the December 1990 freeze will run for another five or six years, until new trees mature. California farmers will eventually completely recover from the effects of the freeze, however, and, if historical weather patterns hold, they will not have to endure another such freeze until around the year 2040.

CALIFORNIA'S DAIRY INDUSTRY—IN A CLASS BY ITSELF

California's milk production represents more than 13 percent of the total U.S. output. Now close to 20,000 billion pounds, the state's dairy output has increased almost 30 percent over the last decade.[11] California's cows are the most productive in the nation: the average California dairy cow gives 18,402 gallons of milk a year.[12] It's a good thing it does: every year the average Californian consumes 96 quarts of milk, 9.5 quarts of skim milk, 1.6 quarts of half-and-half, and 3.2 quarts of yogurt.[13]

But all is not well with the state's dairy farmers. The drought at the start of this decade has made dairymen extremely conservative. The necessity of hauling water to keep herds alive and healthy has created a real economic hardship. Hauling water can cost $70 to $80 a load, a terrible burden for marginal dairy operations. The president of the Western Dairymen's Association recently stated that "the water shortage will undoubtedly put some dairies out of business."[14] To make matters even worse, the drought has driven the price of hay skyward, while market prices for milk have taken a dip at the market level.

Still, the future looks good for dairy farmers for the rest of this century and into the next. Milk and cream, the number one farm products of California for decades, will continue their top ranking into the foreseeable future. By the year 2000, California will be producing a remarkable 5 percent of the nation's milk and dairy products.

FOOD ON THE HOOF: CALIFORNIA LIVESTOCK STROLLS DOWNHILL

California is an important livestock state, but its importance in the overall American market is declining. The number of California beef cows, for instance, has recently declined from 3 percent of the U.S. total to about 2.5 percent.[15] The number of sheep, lambs, and hogs has also declined slowly. The number of chickens sold has diminished without letup over the past ten years. This trend will continue into the foreseeable future.

As land becomes scarcer and more valuable, as the threat of water shortages continues, as the price of hay rises, as public tastes change to lighter foods, the California livestock industry will occupy a less and less important role in California's overall agricultural mix. There will be one exception to this trend in animal farming: turkeys. The number of turkey farmers in California will increase, and turkey production will grow throughout the decade.

GRAPES, RAISINS, AND WINES: BOUNTY FROM VINEYARDS

Products from the vineyards of California—wine, table grapes, and raisins—have been the phenomenal story of the state's agriculture over the past thirty years. Grapes are now the number one crop commodity in California, third behind dairy and meat production among all commodities.

What happens to most of the grapes grown in California? Surprisingly, they become raisins. One of the reasons is that it takes 4.5 pounds of grapes to make a pound of raisins[16]—and raisins rank as one of the most popular snack foods in America.

The California wine industry accounts for almost half of the state's grape usage. Of America's more than 1,200 wineries, 55 percent are in California. California's vineyards and vintners, however, are so productive that they produce 90 percent of all the wine in America. And 95 percent of America's wine exports to other countries are from California.[17]

California's winemakers will no doubt continue to prosper in the coming decade, but they face at least two serious challenges.

Californians are drinking less wine, signaling a trend the nation will follow. Wine consumption in the state has dropped for the past four years. In 1990, the average Californian drank 3.56 gallons of wine, a drop of 28 percent since 1986.[18] In 1991, that figure dropped another 3.1 percent. There are a number of reasons for this decline, including health considerations, tougher drunken-driving laws, and a recessionary economy. The end of the wine cooler craze probably also played a role.

To compound the problem of declining consumption rates for the industry, new federal excise taxes went into effect in 1991, raising the tax from 17 cents a gallon to $1.07 a gallon.[19] This new tax will undoubtedly have a further impact on wine purchases over the next several years.

However, the decline in wine consumption will slow after the next several years, and by the year 2000, consumption will have leveled off to a little more than three gallons annually for the average Californian. The intervening fallout among America vintners will have been minimal.

There has been little public recognition of a second problem facing the wine industry, which is under siege by an enemy so small that it is scarcely visible to the human eye. Its name: Phylloxera. A voracious little plant louse that brought about a terrible devastation in the world's vineyards more than a hundred years ago, Phylloxera is now back in a more virulent form.

The first time Phylloxera made its frightening appearance in the world's vineyards was in the mid-1800s, when it virtually wiped out the great winemakers of Europe. Paradoxically, the microscopic louse, which lives primarily in the soil, arrived in Europe via American plants that were immune to the pest. When these plants arrived in Europe for propagation in nurseries there, they effectively eliminated the French wine industry within a few decades. Only the mass importation of immune American vine stock eventually saved the winemakers of Europe.

Now the hardy pest is back, this time in a version that attacks American vines, and the news is bad. The new mutant strain, known as Biotype B, works slowly, taking three to five years for an infestation to destroy a vineyard. Biotype B first appeared in 1979 on just four vines in Napa. Now as many as 300 acres are infected in Napa County, over 100 acres in Sonoma, and, horrifyingly, about 3,500 acres in Monterey County.[20] The latest, most modern precautions, such as sterilizing farm equipment and workers' boots, only slow its relentless progress.

The effect of Phylloxera Biotype B on California vineyards will be substantial. Each acre affected will have to be sterilized and the vines replaced at an average cost of $13,000. The financial impact between now and the year 2000 could be as great as $250 million, and more than 15,000 acres may be destroyed. The plague will bankrupt some smaller vintners, and there could be some loss of varietal diversity as well before the plague ends.

POLLUTION: A CITY PROBLEM COMES TO THE COUNTRY

In recent years, California farmers have become aware that smog is not restricted to California's urban areas, that poor air quality is not just a big city problem. Bakersfield, for instance, is now the second smoggiest spot in the United States. Fresno's air is dirtier than either New York's or Chicago's. The Sierra Nevada often hides behind a milky veil with a definite brownish cast.[21]

As air quality continues to deteriorate generally across vast sections of California, the state's farmers are beginning to fret. The reason: University of California experiments show that the increasing pollution is beginning to affect crops in the state. In the San Joaquin Valley, for instance, the ozone is reducing yields on cotton by as much as 20 percent, table grapes by 25 percent, oranges by 25 percent.[22] In Fresno, cotton, a major crop, has been headed downhill for twenty years, with air pollution one of the suspected villains.

Air pollution is a vague and nebulous foe for farmers, a foe all too easy to ignore. The damage is not visible to the naked eye. The vegetables, the fruit, the nuts, all look, for the most part, undamaged. The only symptom is that there are fewer of them. When crop yields are mysteriously down, farmers turn to science for the answer, and more and more frequently the answer is coming back—air pollution. A 1990 study shows that growers now lose up to $200 million every year to pollution, with resulting higher prices to consumers.[23]

Experts say there is only one long-range solution to the problem, and that is to clean up the air. Farmers are reluctant environmentalists at best, but some have emerged as activists on this subject. Others hope and expect that the solution will be found in the development of smog-resistant crops. The director of U.C. Riverside's air pollution research program says, "It will take twenty years or more to reduce smog to federal standards." On the other hand, he says, "We can probably find out the genetic basis of resistance and develop crops in seven years."[24] Nonetheless, agriculturists generally recognize that a two-track solution offers the best hope. Air standards will have to be improved or at least sustained while the search for improved trees and plants continues. The farm belt's eight counties in the San Joaquin Valley have already formed a unified air pollution control district to see what can be done to prevent further deterioration of air in the valley. Their effectiveness may be limited: car exhausts, industrial solvents, refinery fumes, and manufacturing exhausts may well be beyond their jurisdiction and outside their actionable range.

By the year 2000, air pollution will pose an even more serious threat to California's agriculture than it does today, costing up to half a billion dollars a year in reduced yields. The effect,

however, will be somewhat ameliorated by the introduction of new largely smog-resistant varieties of trees and plants which will be coming on line during the following decade.

"SUPERBUGS" AND OTHER CATASTROPHES

The recent infestation of a tiny whitefly in the Imperial Valley points up the vulnerability of California's agriculture to unforeseen catastrophes. Dubbed the ''superbug'' by local farmers, this pest is actually a member of the Aleyrodidae family, and probably comes from the Middle East. Possibly it came to California with troops and matériel returning from the Iraq War. Unprecedented in its potential for crop destruction, ''superbug'' has nearly destroyed the entire melon crop, and has seriously damaged other crops, including lettuce, squash, tomatoes, cotton, and alfalfa. Estimates of its probable damage over this growing season run as high as $200 million. This whitefly, never before seen in California, is highly resistant to cold and to chemical treatments.

The surprise appearance of this ''superbug'' is indicative of the unpredictability of the fortunes of California agriculture. Other infestations can occur at any time, from sources unknown at present and in defiance of all known treatments. It is likely, however, that a pesticide can be quickly developed to eradicate this particular pest, and the University of California at Riverside is already heading a task force to find a solution. There will be other surprise infestations between now and the year 2000, but the odds are overwhelming that they will be of a single season's duration. Agricultural scientists in California will bend every effort to find effective treatments for these unforeseen and unpredictable pests as they appear. The cost of not eradicating them quickly is simply too great for California's farmers and consumers.

ALMONDS: WHERE CALIFORNIA RULES THE WORLD

California growers produce a variety of nuts, almost all of which are widely exported to other states as well as overseas. Three of the most popular nuts in America are grown only in California—

almonds, pistachios, and English walnuts. These California exclusives together account for almost $1 billion in sales.[25]

The state's almond industry alone is so dominant that it represents 65 percent of the total world crop. California has approximately 400,000 acres of almond orchards, stretching from Red Bluff in the north to Bakersfield in the south. In 1991, growers were expecting a yield of approximately 655 million pounds of almonds, a crop second only to 1987's record crop of 660 million. The almond is California's largest food export—and the nation's sixth.[26] Americans eat more almonds than pecans, walnuts, or any other tree nut.

In all, more than thirty varieties of almonds are grown in California, including the narrow Carmel and the rounded Mission. A good almond crop depends on cold winters, dry summers, abundant irrigation and, because California almonds are not self-pollinating, a proliferation of cooperative bees.

The odds are that the 1990s will see a generous confluence of these factors and that the almond industry in California will prosper through the decade, maintaining its number-one ranking among the nut tree industries of the state.

THE COMING REVOLUTION IN AGRICULTURE— BIOTECHNOLOGY

The technology of altering biological forms, a science just out of its infancy, has the potential of transforming California agriculture, and agriculture generally, as we move toward and beyond the millennium. The genetic manipulation of crops and farm animals is expanding with greater speed than most people realize. Biotechnology is already affecting agriculture in a number of ways.

- Genetic techniques are being used to grow fish and beef faster.
- Fertilizers and insect resisters are being added to seeds to give them new inherent growing characteristics.
- Genetically engineered seedless grapes and watermelons have been developed and are already on the market.
- Genetically identical purebred bull calves have been produced from embryos made in laboratories.

The contributions of biotechnology to agriculture so far are primitive in comparison with what waits in the near future. Says one biotech pioneer, ''What we are doing now will seem simple and mindless five years from now.''[27] Here are some of the biological ''miracles'' that may not be too far off:

• Genes will be added to protect fruit and nut trees from virus infections that now cost the industry tens of millions of dollars annually.
• The ripening of vegetables will be genetically controlled to make them available in a fresh state throughout the year.
• Apples will be implanted with genes that will keep them from turning brown inside when exposed to air.
• A new ''super tomato'' will be created that will have a higher solids content, will be more difficult to bruise, and can stay on the vine longer without spoiling.
• Popcorn will be created that tastes so ''buttery'' that it will need nothing added.
• Vegetable plants will be developed that can grow and thrive in arid, even polluted, soil.
• There will be flowers with natural fragrances that are two or three times as powerful as at present.
• Insect-repellent broad-leaf vegetable plants will make the use of many insecticides unnecessary.
• Hormones will stimulate milk production in cows by as much as 40 percent.
• Potatoes that have the protein value of meat will be grown in California.
• Large numbers of farm animals, including cattle, sheep, and pigs will be cloned from a single embryo with a uniform quality and standard.
• Artificially created vanilla will replicate all 150 components of natural vanilla.

One difficulty faced by the biotech industry is the red tape necessary to get new creations and products to the marketplace. This problem will clear up as the benefits of bioengineering become more and more apparent.

By the year 2000, new regulations will simplify the muddled process whereby genetically engineered crops, animals, and pesticides are approved. New regulations will treat genetically altered plants and animals the same as those that are conventionally grown and bred. This will significantly affect the types and forms of California crops and livestock as the state's agriculture moves into the next century.

AGRICULTURAL EXPORTS: THE OVERSEAS APPETITE FOR CALIFORNIA FOODS

Almost 25 percent of the state's farmland is planted with crops for export. This year, California food exports will be almost $3.8 billion, an increase of over 30 percent in just the past two years. Japan continues as the leading buyer of California farm products, consuming 29 percent of everything that the state exports.[28] This is almost as much as all of Europe combined. Even so, these exports have not reached the record year of 1981, a full decade ago, when they reached $4.2 billion. The leading exports are cotton, almonds, grapes, oranges, and walnuts.

Throughout the 1990s, California's food exports will continue to grow, as the domestic market becomes less important. By the year 2000, export revenues could reach $7 billion. As Japan gradually and begrudgingly reduces tariff barriers, even for beef and rice, it will become an even more dominant market for California agriculture than at the present time.

FOREIGN OWNERSHIP OF CALIFORNIA FARMLAND

Foreign investors have long been interested in California farmland, first for its potential for operating profit, but also for the potential increase in the value of the land itself. At the present time, over a million acres of California farmland are foreign-owned. This represents only a small fraction of the California total of over 33 million acres. The largest foreign national holder is the United Kingdom, followed by the Netherlands and Germany.[29]

By the end of this decade, foreign ownership of California farmland will more than triple, with over 3 million acres, or close to 10 percent, in foreign hands. The most aggressive purchasers between now and the year 2000 will be the Japanese.

GROWING JOBS IN AGRICULTURE

Employment in California agriculture has grown dramatically over the past several decades, adding more than a hundred thousand jobs since the early 1970s.

By the end of the century, more than 400,000 Californians will be employed in agriculture. The fastest-growing segment will not be in agricultural production itself, but in agricultural services such as veterinary, horticultural, academic, forestry, and chemical. It is difficult to ascertain the exact number of farm workers

TABLE 6-2

CALIFORNIANS EMPLOYED IN AGRICULTURE (IN THOUSANDS)

Year	Agricultural Production	Services*	Total Wage and Salary Employment
1972	208.3	59.8	268.1
1973	222.4	66.6	288.9
1974	236.9	71.2	308.1
1975	243.7	72.0	315.7
1976	248.2	75.3	323.5
1977	241.7	72.9	314.7
1978	245.1	78.9	323.9
1979	253.6	85.0	338.6
1980	261.9	90.3	352.3
1981	258.6	95.8	354.4
1983	250.3	97.1	347.3
1985	232.7	102.7	335.4
1986	220.0	105.6	327.6
1987	227.2	117.8	345.0
1988	235.5	125.1	360.6
1989	233.4	129.1	362.5
1990	232.8	127.3	360.1
1991	232.5	125.6	358.1

*Agricultural services include forestry, but exclude veterinary, other animal, and landscape and horticultural services.

Source: Economic Report of the Governor, 1992.

because their jobs tend to be both transient and transitory, but by the year 2000, increased mechanization will gradually shrink the number of workers required in California's fields and orchards. Despite decades of union activity among the workers, only 9.6 percent are currently unionized. This percentage will also diminish slightly through the decade because of grower opposition, improved working conditions, and job scarcity.

MORE PRODUCTION, FEWER FARMS

Significant changes in the number, size, and character of California's farms have taken place during the past half century. Gross farm income has moved from less than a billion dollars fifty years ago to about $18 billion at the present time. On the other hand, the number of farmers in California has dropped from some 135,000 to just 76,000 over that same time. The average size of farms in California has continued to grow, from 267 acres to well over 400 acres.[30]

This trend of greater production from fewer, larger farms will continue well into the next century.

One reason for this trend is the growing productivity of California farmers, as evidenced by these amazing statistics: a Japanese farmer provides food for 3 people, a Soviet farmer provides food for 11 people, and a California farmer provides food for 114 people. With only 3.5 percent of America's farmers and 3.3 percent of America's farmland, California produces more than half of all of America's nuts and vegetables.[31]

In the year 2000, California, despite fewer farms and a slightly smaller percentage of its total land in farm production, will still dominate American agriculture.

The efficiencies inherent in large-scale farming operation, plus the risks that small farmers run from the vagaries of weather and pricing, will continue gradually to reduce the number of California farms. Still another factor in the shrinking base of farm operators will be the steady encroachment of residential and commercial development.

At the present time, just over 32 percent of California's total land is farmland. By the year 2000, this figure will fall below 30 percent for the first time in California history.

BY THE YEAR 2000:

It is almost certain that:

- California will produce 60 percent of all the vegetables grown in America.
- Total agricultural revenues will be close to $30 billion.
- Dates, figs, pistachios, olives, and kiwis will still be grown only in California.
- Fewer water-intensive crops, such as rice and alfalfa, will be grown in California.
- Biotechnical advances will have greatly reduced the use of fertilizers and insecticides.
- The widely used agricultural pesticide Parathion will be banned altogether because of its effect on farm workers.
- California will still be the largest producer of commercially grown worms.
- Over 10,000 acres of California vineyards will have been destroyed by the new Phylloxera blight.
- California farmers' use of the overall state water supply will be dramatically reduced.
- There will have been at least two major medfly infestations in Southern California.

It is very likely that:

- At least 100,000 acres of farmland and open space will have been lost to suburban sprawl every year.
- The cold weather at the start of this decade will still be remembered as ''the last great freeze.''

- The last remaining commercial farm in the City and County of San Francisco, a three-acre plot, will have disappeared.
- Less than 9 percent of California's farm workers will be unionized.
- More than 15 percent of California's total vegetable production will be grown organically.
- A new fruit, called a "Passion Pop," a cross between the passion fruit and a cold-tolerant weed named "maypop," will be grown and marketed in California.
- Less than 30 percent of California's land surface will still be farmland.
- Avocado stealing will still be the number one agricultural crime in California.

It is even possible that:

- Edible flowers will be an important farm product in California.
- Cattle rustling in California will again be a major industry, with more than 4,000 head stolen annually.
- California will produce more mozzarella cheese than Italy.
- California will have the only large commercial snail ranch in the United States.
- Most broad-leaf vegetable plants grown in California will be insect repellent.
- The typical California dairy cow will give more than 20,000 gallons of milk a year.
- Lettuce the size of a tennis ball, suitable for a single serving, will be a popular staple with California growers and consumers.

7

Where Will All the Water Come From?

From the earliest times, Californians have worried about water and have been willing to pay dearly for it. In the semi-arid desert climate that dominates most of the state, early settlers quickly learned that it rarely rained from May to October and that while the months from December through April were generally wet, even then, the skies could be unpredictable and stingy. Water shortages were seasonal at best, chronic at worst. Ingenuity and resourcefulness came into play almost from the outset. Streams were diverted, rivers were dammed, wells were dug, reservoirs were built, new methods of irrigation were invented. But always, Californians looked prayerfully toward the skies. Their prayers were not always answered.

The first recorded major drought in California came at the end of the nineteenth century. Long and severe, it lasted almost half a decade. By 1903, desperation had set in among Los Angeles's 100,000 citizens.[1] Well pressure all but disappeared, and irrigation had to be shut down in the San Fernando Valley. As a result, the city spent the remainder of the decade building a colossal 250-mile aqueduct from the Owens River in the north that made the explosive growth of Southern California possible. The longest drought in California history came some sixty years later, from 1928 to 1934, again inspiring a great exertion in dam building and river tapping throughout the West. It was another forty-plus years before the next really memorable drought. The years 1976 and 1977 were the driest consecutive years in the recorded history of California.[2] Shasta Lake, the reservoir on which billions of dollars in agriculture depend, was nearly dry, and water rationing was imposed all over the state.

Now, at the start of the last decade of the twentieth century, California is suffering still another great drought. Five consecutive years of inadequate rainfall have left a great deal of ground parched, many rivers dry, some reservoirs close to empty. January, the month when Californians expect greatest rainfall, was only 15 percent of normal in 1991, and even a wet March failed to make up the difference. From the rich farmlands of the Central Valley to the usually snow-covered slopes of the Sierra Nevada and the once-lush gardens of Bel Air, Californians were grappling with what could become the worst drought in California history.

It is possible, of course, that California weather was never intended to sustain the life-styles of 30 million residents and a farming industry that provides a full half of all the nation's fruits and vegetables. What will happen when yet another 5 million people come to California to live by the year 2000?

The Los Angeles Metropolitan Water District, for instance, estimates that if there is a 15 percent shortage in California water supplies in the year 2000, it will cost the region $30 billion and 400,000 to 500,000 jobs.[3] The results for the rest of California would be equally horrendous. If the drought continues, or if there are new droughts, what will the effect be on California's future?

WHY DOES CALIFORNIA HAVE DROUGHTS?

The recent drought, as well as most of the droughts in California history, results from a confluence of unfortunate circumstances. In the late fall and winter months when rain should be falling, cloud banks can usually be seen in satellite pictures moving toward the entire state from far out over the Pacific. But in a drought configuration, the front, as it approaches the continental shelf, moves and swirls northward as a result of high atmospheric pressures that dominate the central part of the state. More often than not, the rain clouds seem to skim the Bay Area and then move north over the upper quarter of California, Oregon, and Washington. In a frustrating ballet of twists and pirouettes, they seem to miss the Sierra Nevada just where the snow pack is needed to create the spring melt-off.[4]

Of course, weather fronts, even in a drought year, do hit California, especially in January and February. But more often than not, they produce little or no rain. Why? Water evaporating from the oceans forms these clouds, usually beginning about 500 feet above the water. Typically only about 2,000 feet thick, they do not contain enough water to produce rain. They are kept from growing thicker by warming air that descends on them from above, acting like a cap on the clouds. Thus, when the seemingly rain-laden clouds drift over the state, they often bring fog and drizzle, but rarely any real precipitation. In a winter when this circumstances occurs with regularity, a drought ensues.

The longest this drought condition has prevailed in recorded California history is six years.[5] It is doubtful, therefore, that the present drought will continue beyond 1992. It may, in fact, be over by the time you read this book.

HOW MUCH WATER WILL CALIFORNIA NEED?

Water use in California between 1972 and 1980 increased by 8 percent. At the start of the past decade it was estimated that the state's water use would increase over the next thirty years, that is, from 1980 to 2010, by only an additional 10%.[6] This slowing anticipated increase was due to growing water conservation and the use of reclaimed water. In fact, there was only a small increase in California's water use in the 1980s. By the year 2000, it is possible that California's water use will increase only marginally.

The five-year drought that has trailed into the start of the 1990s has made Californians water-conscious as never before. Both mandatory rationing and a general state of "water shock" have probably left a lasting impression on the California psyche. It is possible that subsequent years of heavy precipitation will ease the restraints, both regulatory and voluntary, and memories tend to be short. Yet, two major droughts over a fifteen-year period should leave Californians with a lasting legacy of water conservation.

It is estimated that in 1990 California consumed about 34.7 billion acre-feet of water for all uses.[8] The actual total is probably unknowable because of the incredible jumble of water districts, regions, and authorities.

But if California's present 30 million residents plus the additional 5 million newcomers to the state increase the total consumption just a modest 2 percent, California may need some 35.4 billion acre-feet of water annually to satisfy its needs by the year 2000.[9]

Where will all the water come from, who will control it, and who will use it? The answer is complex, confusing, and conjectural.

WATER FROM THE SKIES: THE ULTIMATE HOPE

The odds are overwhelming that the California drought that began in 1987 will not continue far into the 1990s. The prediction of droughts is far from an exact science, but the weather patterns that deprive California of its needed rain almost always terminate in a rainy period. The likelihood that there has been some basic shift in the overall weather pattern that California can expect in the future is remote. Droughts are, by definition, temporary. And when California droughts end, they customarily end not with a whimper, but with a bang. The drought of the 1970s concluded with an extremely wet 1978, followed by an even wetter 1979, followed by a succession of subtropical Pacific storms in 1980 that threatened to float California out to sea. In 1982, the state got three times its normal rainfall, and relentless storms caused billions of dollars of damage.[10]

In the average year between now and the year 2000, California can expect 190 million acre-feet of water to fall on the state from the skies.

Sadly, most of this water will play no role in the overall well-being of the California water supply. Only 71 million acre-feet of the 190 million that falls will find its way into rivers and streams as runoff; the other 119 million acre-feet will either evaporate or go into groundwater. Still, an average rainfall during the 1990s can be expected despite the disappointing way the decade has started off.

Therefore, between now and the year 2000, water from rain and snowfall will put an end to the present drought period and restore average levels in the state's reservoirs.

WATER OUT OF THE GROUND

No one seems to know for certain how many wells there are in California. It is certain, however, that farmers are the principal creators and users of wells in the state. It is also known that during the drought of the 1970s, which lasted only two years, California farmers drilled more than 20,000 new wells before the rains returned. It is also known that in the past half-century, more than 30,000 wells had to be replaced because land collapsed as a result of lowered underground water levels that ripped well casings apart.[11]

Also unknown is the full extent of underground water resources in the state. An estimated 600 million acre-feet is probably sitting in underground water reservoirs in the Central Valley alone. In an average year, more than 10 million acre-feet of rainwater either evaporates or goes into groundwater. But Californians, and especially California farmers, use up a lot of this water. Every day, 125 million gallons are used domestically.[12] Up to 10 million gallons a day may come out of the ground, but no one is quite sure. A tangle of more than 350 water districts, drainage districts, levee districts, and other agencies are supposed to keep track of California's agricultural water resources, yet there is no overall tracking authority keeping an accurate picture of how rapidly water is being pumped out of the ground to replace the scarce surface water supplies.

One thing is known: California's great Central Valley has been sinking as the water table drops. In some areas, the drop has been as much as thirty feet!

The results of this subsiding of the valley have been troublesome. Underground water levels have dropped by as much as 500 feet, and some wells now have to be drilled as deep as 3,000 feet to produce satisfactorily. Levees along the Delta-Mendota Canal have had to be raised, and engineers have been forced to jack up hundreds of bridges and to rebuild miles of highway. Of almost greater concern has been the polluting of some underground aquifers as the runoff of chemically treated water from the region's irrigated fields reaches down into the underground waters.

"We really don't know how much pumping is going on," says Robert Gilliom of the state's geological survey team, "and monitoring what's actually happening is of vital importance."[13] It is possible that at the present time farmers are pumping up many thousands of acre-feet a year more than the aquifers can normally replenish from the surface.

By the year 2000, severe restrictions will be placed on how much water can be removed from California's underground water supply, especially in the Central Valley. As less, not more, water comes from underground California to alleviate the state's water shortage, ever greater stress will be placed on California's ability to manage, store, and conserve its supply of surface water.

As the drought continued in 1991, residential wells were booming in popularity, despite the high cost of drilling and establishing a private well. In the Bay Area, for instance, hundreds of private wells for residential use have been put down. The cost? As much as $20,000 apiece. Said Roy Forster, who operates a well-drilling firm in Marin County, "Business is booming. In fact, it's going crazy. For those who can afford a well, it's a great investment."[14] Municipalities are also beginning to drill more wells for their own use. San Rafael, for instance, recently reopened nine wells and drilled a new one to provide water for the city's parks. Other cities, such as St. Helena in Napa County, are tapping old wells and considering drilling new ones to provide their own residential and commercial users with much-needed water.

By the year 2000, new restrictions will be likely on drilling, both for residential and commercial use. The drillers themselves will be more tightly regulated as to equipment, knowledge, and skills. Approval for drilling sites will require more exacting site studies, pump testing, and water-quality analysis.

WATER FROM NEW DAMS AND RESERVOIRS

There are more than 1,200 major reservoirs in California, and every major river, except one, has been dammed at least once. The Stanislaus River is dammed fourteen times on its short run to the San Joaquin River.[15]

If it were not for this elaborate series of dams and reservoirs, almost all built over the past century, it would be impossible to provide an adequate water supply to Californians, even in a year with above-average rainfall. These dams and reservoirs are, in effect, the storehouses in which water is harvested, held, and later distributed to California residences, businesses, and farms. Yet, the prospect for building new dams and reservoirs to preserve and provide even more water in the years ahead is not good. Cost is one reason: the rising cost of building immense dams and the systems they require is almost prohibitive, especially in the present era of tight state and federal budgets and large deficits.

The other hurdle is equally formidable: environmentalism. Groups associated with environmental causes have almost always opposed the damming of rivers and streams. The Sierra Club and John Muir violently opposed the building of the Hetch-Hetchy Dam in the Yosemite Valley which now provides water for some three million Californians.

More recently, construction of the Buckhorn Canyon Dam has been frustrated. The board of directors of the East Bay Municipal Utility District recommended damming the Buckhorn to create a reservoir holding enough water to serve roughly 160,000 families of five for a year. The Sierra Club, however, ran a slate of directors opposing the reservoir that was elected to office after a highly publicized campaign in early 1991. It now appears extremely unlikely that the dam will ever be built.

Augmenting this difficulty is the way in which public opinion has turned against the construction of dams, once regarded as the basic accepted technique of water capture. A recent poll by the *Los Angeles Times* shows that building dams and reservoirs would be approved by only 26 percent of Californians; it ranked third behind desalinization and conservation/rationing as the desired tactic for solving California's water problem.[17]

The weapon of the environmental impact study alone is enough to discourage most advocates of dam construction. As a result, the most basic and effective method of capturing and storing water in California is probably no longer available for future development.

Unless continued drought completely reorders the priorities of California's environmental establishment, an extremely unlikely prospect, no major new dams or reservoirs will be under construction in California before the end of the century.

A NEW KIND OF DAM

It is likely that in the 1990s a great deal of creativity will be used to capture and conserve water. Witness the "world's largest inflatable rubber dam" now used at Alameda Creek in Fremont. The inflatable dam is 291 feet long and, when filled with air, creates a 13-foot-high dam across the river which, in turn, creates a 50-million-gallon temporary lake.[18] The stored water can be pumped into a dozen quarry ponds and wells in the area. Built by a Japanese firm, the immense rubber dam is inflated by two air compressors whenever there is sufficient rain to justify the effort. Installed just two years ago, it is the third rubber dam employed by the district; two smaller versions have been operating downstream for a number of years. It is almost impervious to vandalism; armor-plated ceramic chips are impregnated into its ¾-inch-thick walls, making it the first bullet-proof rubber dam in the world.

The success of California's first rubber dams will no doubt mean that other such dams will be used in the years ahead, and that other inventive solutions employing new technology can be expected.

WATER FROM A CHANGING AGRICULTURE

An estimated 83 percent of all the water used in California is used to irrigate agricultural crops. The remaining 17 percent is used for residential, industrial, and commercial purposes.[19] Until very recently, this dominant use of the state's water supply by California farmers was seldom questioned, but now proponents of changes in priorities in water distribution are speaking out.

One critic, Marc Reisner, author of *Overtapped Oasis*, estimates that if California farmers used 10 percent less water and that water could be diverted to cities and urban areas, the state's water supply would support as many as 27 million new Californians.[20] Attractive as that thought might be to some, it gives no indication of the difficulty of reducing agricultural usage or in transferring such water from farm to city. Both are fraught with political, as well as physical problems. Nevertheless, there will be mounting pressure on California agriculture to do everything possible to reduce consumption of California water. The following changes in water use policy may be expected by the end of the century:

- **Tighten the qualifications for the use of federally subsidized irrigation water.** Some believe that legal loopholes meant for small family farms are being used by large corporate farms in California. These loopholes, it is claimed, permit these large farms to obtain water for a fraction of its true cost and thus to squander water, or at least to make profligate use of water, which would not otherwise be permitted.
- **Eliminate the use of subsidized water to grow crops that the government considers surplus.** Some farmers use low-cost water to raise crops for which they later receive federal price-support payments.
- **Reduce the growing of relatively low-value crops that require high water use.** Irrigated pastureland for sheep and cattle, for example, uses about one-eighth of the state's total water supply in the average year, yet represents only 1/6,000th of the state's overall economy.[21]
- **Restrict the growth of the top three water-using crops: rice, alfalfa, cotton.** Some water experts say that alfalfa alone uses more water annually than residents of the Los Angeles and San Francisco areas combined.
- **Reduce the amount of land that is pre-irrigated for annual crops.** A number of critics claim that the technique of pre-moisturing land before planting wastes water.

• **In times of drought or emergency, give preference in water allocation to perennial crops.** The use of surface water could be allocated in drought times to perennial crops such as fruit trees and grapevines to preserve their future well-being. At the same time, water allocated to annual crops, such as lettuce and broccoli, which can be reestablished in a short time in subsequent years, could be cut back.

There is no question that California agriculture's big thirst is no longer a sacred cow. Until now, debates over water use have been on a largely regional basis, that is, Northern California versus Southern California, and county versus city. But now, quite suddenly, agriculture is on the defensive; its dominant use of the state's water is being challenged and resented as residential users face quota reductions. One respected state senator has stated unequivocally that future urban water demands would come "from a reallocation of water conserved by agriculture."[22]

By the year 2000, California agriculture can be expected to reduce its use of the state's total water supply by from 5 to 10 percent in response to voter pressure and state regulatory and legislative action.

WATER FROM THE SEA: THE EXPENSIVE ANSWER

The truth of the matter is that there has never been a real water shortage in California, nor will there ever be one. Not as long as California has a 1,200-mile coastline on the Pacific Ocean. Within the state's continental limits is more water than the state could ever use. The problem, of course, is in the science and the cost of making that water useful. Happily, the technology of desalination has made excellent strides in recent years. Entire countries, such as Saudi Arabia, now have assured themselves of a permanent supply of fresh water through the installation of major desalination plants.

Typically, seawater contains 35,000 parts per million of dissolved minerals. Brackish water has up to 10,000 ppm. Water is deemed fit to drink at 500 ppm.[23] The earliest method of reducing minerals in water, called "distillation," places ocean water in a vacuum, then heats it to form a fresh-water vapor, which then condenses into drinking water. In a more recent method called "reverse osmosis," artificial pressure forces sea water through a semipermeable membrane that permits only water molecules to pass through, leaving the salt that was in the water on the other side of the membrane.

Robert Castle, senior engineer for the Marin Municipal Water District, says emphatically that "desalination is doable. It's drought-proof. It can't be cut off by someone outside the county."[24] The District, which serves the southern half of Marin County, expects to raise more than $55 million to build its own major desalting plant. A pilot test of various designs and configurations is already under way. Santa Barbara, hard hit by the drought, has already contracted for construction of a $25 million desalination plant that they expect to provide a full one-third of the the city's water by the mid-1990s. Catalina Island is California's first area to be supplied with desalinated water, by virtue of its new $3 million plant in Avalon.[25]

Both Marin and Santa Barbara are logical candidates for desalination plants, not only because both suffer severely from droughts, but because they both depend on local water sources, with systems that are not tied into a larger network of pipes. Desalinated water can thus be easily distributed within their own communities. The Marin and Santa Barbara plants will be similar in size, producing 5,000 acre-feet annually. The Marin plant, however, will cost twice as much because it will be a permanent fixture, whereas the Santa Barbara plant will be housed in trailers. The Marin plant will also produce purer water, with an extremely low ppm of 100.[26]

Desalination plants have several disadvantages. The first is cost. An acre-foot of desalinated water contains 326,000 gallons, roughly the amount of water that two average single-family homes consume in a year. A single acre-foot costs roughly $2,000, which is vastly more expensive than water from conventional sources. As a result, communities in both Marin and Santa Barbara will have about a 25 percent increase in their water bills.[27] The second disadvantage of desalination is that it is energy-intensive. Desalination that boils the seawater tends to consume electricity voraciously. Reverse-osmosis plants are about 50 percent less energy-intensive, but still use large amounts of electricity.

Nonetheless, desalination plants are solving water shortages in many parts of the world. Saudi Arabia's state-owned Water Conversion Corporation produces an amazing 5,000 million gallons of desalinated water a day. Over the next three years, the Bechtel Corporation will complete $7.5 billion worth of additional desalination operations in the Middle East, to be completed by the middle of the decade. The United States itself now has 12 percent of the total capacity of desalination in the entire world.[28] Desalination is a common means of producing potable water throughout the Caribbean.

Additional desalination plants will be built in California by the year 2000. In addition to Marin and Santa Barbara, Morro Bay, Ventura, Monterey, Oxnard, San Diego, and Los Angeles are logical locations for desalination facilities. Desalination has a definite future in California.

WATER FROM RESTRICTED USAGE

Perhaps the first and easiest reaction to any California water shortage is to ration its use. Usually, the rationing has been voluntary, with authorities urging consumers in specific areas to restrict their usage by a given percent. Throughout the drought of the 1970s, almost all rationing was stated in voluntary percentages, and the results were salutary. But in the drought of the 1980s and 1990s, voluntary efforts were deemed inadequate almost everywhere.

One of the most restrictive water rationing plans ever inflicted on a community was imposed in Marin County. In February of 1991, the Marin Municipal Water District adopted rationing standards that allowed only fifty gallons per resident, barely a survival ration in terms of contemporary living standards.

The prize for the most severe water rationing plan, however, belongs to Orange Cove, a small town in the San Joaquin Valley. Orange Cove asked its citizens to limit themselves to ten gallons a day, enough to cook or bathe, but not both.[29] The harshness of this plan was softened by the fact that houses in Orange Cove have no water meters.

Less arduous, more livable rationing restrictions have been placed on the residents of Los Angeles, San Francisco, and other communities. Generally, the goal is to limit usage to about 300 gallons, down from a statewide average of about 450 gallons. The goal of 300 gallons daily is both reasonable and attainable.

Mandated percentage cuts in usage are also a popular method of encouraging reduced usage. Los Angeles, earlier in the year, mandated a 15 percent cut in household use from the base year of 1986. San Francisco and other Hetch-Hetchy districts ordered a cut of 33 percent based on the year 1987. One problem, of course, with percentage cuts is that they penalize those households that have had the history of lowest water consumption.

Other techniques popularly employed in California include forbidding the watering of lawns, the washing of cars, the sprinkling of golf course fairways, and the filling of swimming pools and hot tubs.

Mandatory cutbacks on a numerical basis entail a number of inherent difficulties. For instance, in urban areas a majority of residents are customarily renters, so that the tenant is responsible for the conservation, but the financial penalty is on the landlord. Another problem is that not all communities have metered homes. Houses in Sacramento, for instance, have no meters, so it is impossible to measure household performance and to impose penalties.

Mandatory water cuts are widely unpopular, even in a time of drought emergency. As soon as normal rainfall returns, popular pressures usually force removal of imposed restraints. Yet, there is now a growing awareness that some long-range consumer plan will be required.

THE FUTURE OF CLOUD SEEDING

At the present time, nineteen cloud-seeding projects are under way in California, all designed to induce the sometimes stingy clouds over the state to yield their rain and snow. A number of these projects have been under way for over a decade, and their longevity indicates the confidence their sponsors have in their effectiveness.

It has been more than four decades since General Electric scientists first discovered that seeding certain kinds of clouds with silver-iodide or dry ice crystals provoked precipitation. Experts almost all agree that cloud-seeding works. No one has ever suggested that it is the answer to drought, but it can be used to augment normal rainfall by from 5 to 15 percent in a given year in certain areas.

The Sacramento Municipal Utility District, seeding with ground-based generators rather than planes, produces enough additional water for 16,000 households a year.[30]

The growing acceptance of seeding is evident in the fact that almost fifty countries plan to use the technique to augment their normal rainfall. Recently, the Los Angeles County Board of Supervisors overcame former reservations about the technique and adopted a cloud-seeding resolution, urging that "a coordinated effort needs to be spearheaded at the state level."[31]

By the end of the century, a statewide program of seeding clouds will be in place for additional precipitation in dozens of areas. This program will doubtless produce a flurry of lawsuits by environmentalists who feel that forcing Mother Nature isn't nice, and by communities and counties that will argue that cloud seeding in another area has deprived them of their normal share of rainfall.

ALLOCATING WATER BY QUALITY: MORE WATER, WORSE WATER?

If water becomes scarcer in California in the years ahead, there may well be pressure to lower existing standards of water quality for various uses. Standards for drinking water will, however, be carefully preserved; the Federal Safe Drinking Water Act of 1974 will see to that.[32] Nevertheless, it may be that water that is slightly brackish, or of poorer quality, will be deemed suitable for certain kinds of agricultural and industrial use. Already under discussion is a plan to ease Environmental Protection Agency restrictions against the use of treated water in streams. Easing these restrictions would increase water flow in rivers and streams and cool water temperatures to increase the survival rate of fish and wild life.

By putting lower-grade water to less demanding use, water of higher quality will become available for use where higher standards are required. Look for greater planning in the years ahead directed at putting water to its optimal use by quality grade and type.

RECLAIMED WATER: REUSING WHAT WE ALREADY HAVE

Techniques are improving every year for reclaiming used water and making it serviceable for other purposes. One of the most common reclamation practices is the cleansing of waste water from sewage treatment plants. The Orange County Water District, for instance, operates a 15-million-gallon-per-day reverse-osmosis plant in Fountain Valley that cleans waste water and reuses it for a variety of purposes, including injecting it into the ground as a barrier between underground reservoirs and ocean water. Much of the water then flows inland and is pumped out again for use in the water system.[33]

In the East Bay, water authorities are considering using treated sewer water to supply Chevron at its Richmond oil refinery cooling tank, thus allowing diversion of industrial water to other uses. There is also a plan to use treated nonpotable water from Lake Chabot in San Leandro to irrigate local golf courses.

Look for new techniques and new technology to be in place by the end of the decade that will permit communities and water districts to reclaim used water to a greater degree than is now possible. In some areas, the same water will be used three and four times before it is surrendered to the soil and the ocean.

WATER C.O.D.

In future droughts, one startling option will be available to coastal communities desperate for water: they will be able to buy water on the open market and have it shipped in. In March of 1991, the Goleta Water District, in the Santa Barbara area, contracted with a company to ship Canadian water to the area by supertanker, the first time such a drastic action was ever taken in the United States. Faced with its reservoir running dry, Goleta's 70,000 residents and its agricultural businesses were facing disaster. The district made plans to ship an estimated 7,500 acre-feet of water a year from British Columbia, an area that averages more than 150 inches of rainfall a year, compared with Goleta's 6 inches. Ships loaded with Canadian water would dock near Goleta and be unloaded by a pipeline to the district's treatment plant. The water would then be distributed through normal channels. The project, designed to run for seven years, was expected to cost $22.5 million annually.[34] The higher costs would be passed along to water users.

The idea of bringing water in by tanker is not completely new. Bulk water has been tankered to parched areas in the Caribbean at various times and was also shipped to the U.S. troops serving in the Persian Gulf.

Even though the cost of tankered water is extremely high, it offers a sensible alternative to drought-stricken areas that are accessible by sea. Tankered water will cost between $2,300 and $4,000 per acre-foot, some ten times what farmers are accustomed to paying and more than twice what householders are usually charged.[35]

Yet, future major droughts may require drastic solutions, and water shipped by sea will offer a tempting alternative to communities in desperate straits.

ESTABLISHING A MARKET SYSTEM FOR WATER

The desalinated water that will be produced in Santa Barbara will cost $2,000 per acre-foot. Residential water in San Francisco costs about $280 per acre-foot. Farmers in the north San Joaquin Valley obtain irrigation water for $12 per acre-foot. The question of what water should cost Californians and what rates are fair for different segments of the economy is being raised now as never before.

Why shouldn't the demand for water in California be controlled by pricing? Why shouldn't water cost more when it's scarce, less when it's abundant? In the land of the market economy, the market water-system has never been fully tried. Perhaps it never will be, for governments and bureaucracies have little or no experience with market pricing for their products and services. Yet, there is little question that more costly water would result in reduced demand.

San Francisco, along with several other cities and areas in California, is already considering moving to a modified market-usage system to reduce water consumption. City Water Department Manager John Mullane suggests, "If you have a 300-gallon allotment, we may have an increasing rate structure that says for the first 200 gallons you pay X and for the next 100 gallons you pay Y. As you use more, you pay more."[36]

As sensible as a real market system might be to reduce demand in times of shortage, there is little likelihood that it will be implemented to any great degree in California. It would simply be too difficult to justify politically, in face of the accusation that it would work a hardship on the less affluent segments of the population. Do not look for any version of market-pricing to help solve the California water problem by the year 2000 or anytime thereafter.

THE END OF "WATER ON DEMAND"

Many Californians use water from local sources that they control. But huge areas have been developed and put into agriculture only because of water provided by huge state delivery systems, such as Hetch-Hetchy, the federal Central Valley Water Project, and the State Water Project. Many of these areas grew to their present size because farmers assumed that the state could provide as much water as was needed, for whatever purpose was required, for virtually whatever price was desired. This hypothesis was based on the theory that all droughts would be short-lived, or, as one water observer remarked, "that serious droughts were illegal." Former Governor Jerry Brown's deputy water director once described the system by saying, "We were delivering water literally on demand."[37]

THE CONTENDING FORCES

The struggle to benefit from California's water supply will be primarily a three-way battle between farmers, business interests, and

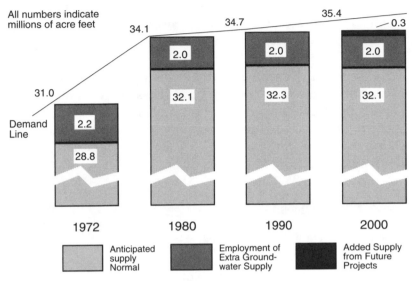

FIGURE 7-1
WATER DEMAND AND SUPPLY IN CALIFORNIA

Source: California Department of Water Resources.

environmentalists. General consumers will sometimes seem lost in the welter of words and lawsuits. No matter who eventually triumphs, the California Department of Water Resources predicts that by the year 2000 there could well be a shortfall in the water supply for all constituencies.

It is likely, however, that this official forecast will turn out to have been too pessimistic. If the California drought ends, as it should; and if the state enters a sustained rainy period, as history indicates it will; and if the forces contending for the supply reach a meaningful compromise, as they must; and if the U.S. Congress passes the needed legislation to revamp the Central Valley Water Project as it surely will; then California's water supply between now and the year 2000 could be more than adequate.

New policy will have to be developed to protect against overuse of water in good years and to assure fair and equitable distribution during times of drought. This policy will have to resolve disputes between Northern California, where most of the water is generated and stored, and Southern and Central California, where most of the water is used. It will have to balance urban and residential use against the demands of agriculture. And it will have to permit the distribution and exchange of water between different districts and between state and federal sources.

In the main, future state water policy will require ongoing conservation measures through good times and bad, and it will require on a continuing basis the kind of water-banking and water-marketing that usually are practiced only in times of a shortage. Before the year 2000, look for important new legislation and regulation aimed at achieving both goals.

BY THE YEAR 2000:

It is almost certain that:

- The state legislature will operate a continuous "water bank" that will reimburse farmers who use low-cost water to take their land for water-intensive crops out of production. The water will then be resold to needy communities at a higher cost.
- It will be illegal to hook up a new house to its water supply without installing a meter.
- Low-flow toilets and showers will be mandatory for all new and remodeled homes throughout California.
- There will be new restrictions and close monitoring of water taken by well usage.
- There will be new desalinization plants in Santa Barbara and Marin, possibly in Monterey, San Diego, San Luis Obispo, and Los Angeles.
- The price of water will double for farmers and triple for home consumers.

It is quite likely that:

- No major new dams or reservoirs will be built in California.
- Growing of water-intensive agricultural products will be dramatically reduced.

- The drip method of irrigation will become mandatory for the growing of many fruits and vegetables.
- ''Gray water'' home filtering systems, which enable the owner to reuse tap and bath water for garden and lawn use, will be used increasingly.
- The drought of 1989-1992 will be only a dim memory.
- A new drought will be under way.

It is even possible that:

- An underground water pipeline from Alaska to California will be under construction.
- Many homes in California will be equipped with faucet regulators that can adjust and limit the flow of water at the tap, depending on the severity of drought conditions.
- Water in San Francisco will be augmented by the discovery of substantial aquifers beneath the city.
- As many as a dozen rubber inflatable dams will be in place on various California rivers.
- Cloud-seeding will be adding up to 5% additional precipitation in California.
- The San Diego desalination plant will be built in Mexico to avoid U.S. and California regulatory problems.

The Healthiest Californians

Managing and improving the health of 30 million Californians is a massive undertaking, a huge enterprise, a major industry. California has more hospitals than Sweden, more surgeons than Canada, and health costs that are higher than the defense budget of Great Britain.

California has more than 75,000 doctors, 19,000 dentists, 250,000 nurses, and 3,246 medical and nursing facilities. Spending on health care currently accounts for almost 12 percent of the entire state gross product.[1] Yet, as impressive as these numbers are, they will seem modest when compared with the health requirements of Californians at the turn of the century. With five million more people residing in the state, with Californians living longer than ever, with the science of medicine reaching new levels of sophistication, the cost and complexity of delivering health services in California will skyrocket.

IT WILL BE MORE EXPENSIVE TO BE SICK IN CALIFORNIA

Californians now spend more per person on health care than residents of any other state except Massachusetts. California spending for medical services totaled $2,894 a person in 1990, up from $1,286 just ten years ago.[2]

It is projected that spending on health for each Californian will increase to more than $6,500 by the year 2000.

The two basic reasons why California is a costly place in which to be ill are the high charges of California doctors and the expense of staying in California hospitals. The last time California surgical costs were compared with the national average, California charges were considerably higher. A typical appendectomy, for instance, cost $5,090 across the U.S., but in California an appendectomy cost an average of $7,480. At the same time, the average cost of a day in a typical U.S. hospital was $538; in California the average cost was $741.[3]

One of the most commonly cited reasons for the high cost of medical services in California is the startlingly high rates of medical malpractice insurance in the state, which physicians and institutions pass along to patients in their pricing. There is no reason to believe that anything will happen to remedy this situation in the 1990s.

In all likelihood, the disparity in the cost of California medical treatment will be even greater by the year 2000. California will continue to be a very expensive place in which to be ill. It may, in fact, pass Massachusetts to become number one in health costs per capita.

THE HEALTH BUSINESS – A BOOM INDUSTRY!

The health-care sector of the California economy has never felt better. The health industry—actually, the ill-health industry—has been growing continuously in the state even throughout the recent recession, and it will continue to grow at an ever accelerating pace in the years ahead. As the California population continues to expand at a 500,000 plus annual pace, and as the average California life span continues to increase, the need for medical services will expand dramatically and the medical sector will become an employment juggernaut.

For the twelve months ending January 1990, for instance, manufacturing dropped almost half a million workers. But in that same period, health services actually added 600,000 jobs, more than offsetting the combined losses in every manufacturing category.[4] The industry has far from topped out. The average vacancy rate for nurses in California is running between 9 and 10 percent. There are also serious shortages of radiology technicians, occupational and physical therapists, and other skilled, highly paid health professionals.

The share of the gross national product taken by health care has risen from 5 percent in the 1940s to more than 12 percent today. It could reach 20 percent early in the next century. The Bureau of Labor Statistics forecasts that seven of the ten fastest-growing occupations through the year 2000 will be in the health-care field.

In California, the state Employment Development Commission predicts that between 1988 and the end of the century, employment of nurses will grow by 48 percent, home health-care aides by 76 percent, medical records technicians by 73 percent, physical therapy assistants by 62 percent, and medical assistants by 60 percent. Employment in all health occupations will grow by 32 percent.[5] Health, already big business in California, will be one of the true boom industries of the 1990s.

CALIFORNIANS AT BIRTH—DOING WELL AND GETTING BETTER

At the present time, California has the tenth lowest infant mortality rate in the nation. The national rate is 10.4 deaths per 1,000 infants born. The California rate is 8.8. This low figure is consistent for whites, Hispanics, and Asians. Black infant mortality rates, however, are almost twice as high as those of the other groups. The low overall rate for California persists in spite of some troubling facts about California mothers and their offspring.[6]

- 5.7 percent of California mothers had no prenatal care or had care only in the last stages of pregnancy.
- 0.9 percent of California babies are born outside of a hospital.
- 24 percent of California mothers are not married.
- 11 percent of California mothers are teenagers.
- 23 percent of California children are delivered by Caesarean section.
- 6 percent of California children are born with a birth weight below 2,500 grams.

The relatively low incidence of infant mortality in California will be even more pronounced by the end of this decade. The

present state and volunteer programs to bring prenatal care to expectant mothers, in addition to increased medical skills in the field of obstetrics, will further reduce the incidence of infant death. The mortality rate in California can be expected to drop to 7.5 per 1,000 or lower by the year 2000.

HOSPITAL MERGERS AND SHAKEUPS

The existing system of hospitals in California will undergo marked change by the end of the 1990s. One reason is the remarkable shift in recent years in length of hospital stays. Patients now stay in California hospitals for ever-decreasing periods of time for most operations and ailments. The typical patient now stays just 5.7 days in a General Acute Care hospital in California, almost half of what it was two decades ago. The daily average cost of a hospital stay, on the other hand, has almost tripled in the past decade. As a result, the occupancy rate at California's 512 G.A.C. hospitals is down to 54 percent. For all hospitals in the state, the occupancy rate declined from 74 percent in 1960 to 57 percent in 1990.[7]

California has lost thirty-three public hospitals since 1965. They include the Shasta General Hospital in Redding and hospitals in Humboldt, Lassen, Modoc, Sutter, and Tulare counties. Hospitals in Mendocino, Yolo, Tuolumne, Modesto, and Trinity counties are now on the endangered list. The National Association for Hospital Development predicts that 40 percent of all hospitals in the United States will be closed by the year 2000.[8]

By the year 2000, many new hospitals will be built to accommodate the residents of burgeoning new residential areas in the suburbs and exurbs. But dozens of existing hospitals in California will be forced to shut down, merge, or convert to nursing homes.

The rising proportion of elderly in the California population will require extensive concentration by the medical profession on geriatric medicine and extended health care. Hospitals will concentrate more and more on caring for the elderly, with many of them converting exclusively to treating the aged. Nursing homes and health centers for the elderly will spring up in all metropolitan and suburban areas. Nursing homes alone will nearly double by the year 2000. Hospices for the incurably ill and for the extremely aged will be an increasingly prominent part of the state's health-care system.

As the California population ages, and as the numbers of extremely elderly grow, insurance companies will respond to demand and offer long-term policies to pay for extended care. And because elderly voters will constitute a powerful political force, both Medicare and Medicaid will increase their support for long-term elderly care both in hospitals and in alternative-care facilities.

New for-profit hospital chains will spread throughout California, buying up and taking over independent and nonprofit hospitals. Less "hospitals" as they now exist, these institutions will be "super-meds," offering a wide variety of medical services, including normal hospitalization and operating facilities, pharmacies, walk-in clinics, dental services, mental illness treatment centers, and health insurance offices. They may also offer remote, off-the-premises diagnostics through a central computer. Remote computer monitoring of a patient's blood pressure, temperature, and other vital signs will be offered by these "mega-hospitals" for patients who prefer to stay at home.

At least two chains of this new kind of health center will be operating in California by the end of the century, with more to come in the years ahead.

CALIFORNIA'S LOW CANCER RATE WILL CONTINUE

For reasons that are not clear, California's overall cancer rate is significantly lower than that of the nation for a great many forms of the disease. The lower rate is consistent among both sexes and for all races in the five principal major California regions. Overall, the cancer rate for California is more than 10 percent below the nationwide rate.

Of 38 major types of cancer, the overall age-adjusted rate for California is 333 cases per 100,000 population, as opposed to 357 cases nationally.[9] There are some exceptions by type. For instance, cervical cancer among women in California was higher than the national average, while prostate cancer among men was much lower than the rate nationally. There are also some differences within the various regions of California. The overall cancer rate for the San Francisco Bay Area is higher than that of the Los Angeles area, for instance. The Central Valley has a higher incidence of lung cancer than any of the other state areas. Yet, the pattern of low cancer rate is consistent throughout California and for almost all types of the disease.

The most immediate explanation for the low cancer rates in California is that the state has a disproportionately high percentage of Asians and Hispanics in its population. Both Asians and Hispanics have better diets than the general population, that is, they generally eat less meat and more vegetables and fruits. Also, members of both minorities have lower smoking rates than the general population and therefore can be expected to have less lung cancer.

As the percentage of Asians and Hispanics dramatically increases in California between now and the year 2000, cancer rates will continue to drop against the national average. This will be especially true for cancers attributable to diet such as stomach and colon cancer.

HIGH-TECH MEDICINE IS AROUND THE CORNER

Amazing progress will be made in the next ten years in a wide variety of medical specialities, and in the treatment and cure of many human ailments. Here are some of the medical advancements that will be available to Californians:

• New varieties of imaging machines will make it possible to find and analyze tumors, disease, and injuries with far more accuracy than is now possible.

- Genuine advances will be made in the understanding and treatment of Alzheimer's disease, Downs syndrome, and diseases for which there is now no effective treatment.
- Biotechnology—gene engineering—will be a big factor in improved health care. "Monoclonal antibodies" will increasingly replace radiation and chemotherapy for the treatment of cancer and tumors. Genetically altered cells will permit the carrying of the body's own anti-disease substances directly to the disease site.
- New and improved vaccines will be available to deal with meningitis, gonorrhea, whooping cough, influenza, hepatitis, chicken pox, herpes, malaria, and rabies.
- Scientists will be able to grow nerve tissue and, in some cases, replace damaged or missing brain cells.
- New ways will be found to protect the brain during stroke until fresh supplies of blood and glucose can reach it.
- Techniques will be available to regenerate parts of the nervous system. Treatment for back injuries and ruptured disks will be greatly advanced.
- Arthritis and related disorders will be controlled by dramatic new treatments, possibly including control of the body's immune system to eliminate the basic cause of arthritis.
- Worn-out and arthritic joints will be renewed by lubricating bone surfaces with laboratory-enhanced natural body fluids.
- Coronary bypass operations will more and more be replaced by the use of catheters and lasers to open clogged arteries.
- Heart attack victims will be treated with special enzymes designed to break up clots, limiting heart damage, and even, in some cases, undoing heart damage. New classes of drugs will replace digitalis for stimulating heart function.
- Genetic screening will be employed to determine in advance an individual's susceptibility to carcinogens and other health hazards.

These are not medical visions of the far future. All of these advancements in the treatment and care of specific human ailments will be available to Californians by, or very near, the year 2000.

CALIFORNIANS GETTING BY—WITH A LITTLE HELP

A pin, a tube, a wire, a valve, a plastic hip—one in twenty Californians has been implanted with some kind of medical device to help them keep going. Fixation devices, such as screws, plates, and wires are the most common implants, and more than half of all implants are in or below the hip. Among the most common replacement implants in Californians are:[10]

- Artificial eye lenses, 310,000. Half are in people over 75 years of age.
- Artificial joints, 2 million. One-third are knee replacements; half are hips.
- Heart valves, 32,000.
- Pacemakers, 78,000.
- Eardrum tubes, 12,500; half in children age 5 or younger.
- Dental implants, 39,000.
- Silicone implants, mostly breasts, 78,000.

With technology rapidly improving, implants will be in even wider use by the year 2000. As medical science learns more about compatibility and infection problems, a far wider range of implants will be available to keep Californians functioning. Most likely, these will include artificial kidneys and other vital organs. By the start of the next century, one in fifteen Californians will have some kind of artificial aid implanted in his or her body.

BODY PARTS OF THE FUTURE

The array of additional body parts to be available soon after the turn of the century will be impressive. Medical science has already provided a trove of highly sophisticated spare parts for the human body. They include joints (finger, knee, elbow, hip, wrists, and ankle), tendons, legs, feet, silicone ears and noses, eye sockets, ocular lenses, heart valves (seven different types), heart pacemakers, and tooth implants. Bioengineers are now predicting that in the not-too-distant future, artificial components will be able to take the place of virtually any portion of the human body except the brain.

After the year 2000, it is anticipated that a vast array of new body parts will be commonly used by surgeons to replace defective or missing human organs and parts.

Recently, molecular biologists have discovered dozens of previously unknown proteins, called growth factors, that stimulate the growth of cells and prod them into changing their form and function. Medical researchers are capitalizing on this newly acquired skill to build artificial organs. An artificial liver will be used in clinical trials by the end of this decade. Bioengineers will be creating new kinds of prostheses that interact with nerves and even brain cells. Here are some of the miracles that medical science will have to work with some time early in the twenty-first century:

- **Skin.** Replacement skin, cultured from human skin cells, will be available. Sheets of new skin big enough to cover a man will be grown in the laboratory and used by surgeons on burn victims.
- **Organoids.** Liver, pancreas, and other organs will be grown from human cells on a sponge-like polymer scaffold and implanted by surgeons.
- **Cartilage.** Like organoids, human cartilage cells will be grown in the lab and will be available in the form of replacement ears, noses, and joints.
- **Lungs.** A plastic device that exchanges oxygen with blood will be available for placement in blood vessels and will be able to handle 50 percent of the lungs' work.
- **Bone.** Temporary artificial bones will stimulate the growth of real bones to take their place.
- **Eyes.** A light-sensitive device with electrodes leading to the brain will crudely simulate vision.
- **Nerve chips.** Microchips, embedded surgically in the stump of a limb, will pick up impulses from nerve fibers leading from the brain and transmit them to an external computer to control an artificial limb.
- **Blood.** Artificial and synthetic blood, half as thick as real blood, will be used to supply oxygen to certain tissues during operations and to unclog blocked blood vessels.

Early versions of some of these advancements will be available to California doctors by the year 2000. The effectiveness and speed of research to create these medical wonders will depend on congressional funding and the ability of the scientific community to work together to achieve specific goals.

NEW MOMS OVER FIFTY AND OTHER UNLIKELY EVENTS

For the first million years or so of human reproduction, there was only one way to make a baby. That all changed with the procedure known as *in vitro* fertilization, in which eggs are removed from the ovaries, mixed with sperm in the laboratory, allowed to develop into embryos and then inserted into the uterus. Since 1978, some 20,000 babies have been born using this technique.[11] Variations on and improvements in the IVF procedure are coming with ever-increasing rapidity.

One of the latest developments will permit women who are many years into menopause to give birth. Menopause, which shuts down the release of eggs from the ovary, customarily leaves the other reproductive organs in viable condition. By the year 2000, a woman will routinely be able to become pregnant using someone else's eggs implanted in her uterus. A medical team at the University of Southern California has already successfully impregnated six of seven postmenopausal women using these techniques, and four of them gave birth to healthy offspring.[12] The experiment demonstrates that many women become infertile not because their uteruses are too old, but because their ovaries are.

It will soon be possible through the use of this technique for women in their late forties and fifties to bear children. This raises the specter in the next century of women in their seventies attending the high school graduations, not of their grandchildren, but of their own children.

Other remarkable advances in procreation as well as in birth prevention will be commonplace by the next century. A male contraceptive that works like the female birth-control pill will be in use. Testesterone enanthate, a synthetic variant of a naturally occurring hormone will be used by injection by men desiring safe, effective, and reversible contraception. It may also be available as a pill.

California will be the first state to test RU-486, the controversial "abortion pill," sometimes called the "morning after" contraception pill.

Now legal in France, the abortion pill has already been deemed safe and effective by many American medical authorities, and the California Medical Association has already recommended putting it into test. By the end of the decade, it will be readily available throughout the state.

Surgery on unborn infants will be quite common throughout the state by the year 2000. Prenatal examination and diagnosis of problems in infants in the womb will reach a point of surprising sophistication by the end of the decade. Simple surgical procedures to correct certain malformations and to assist proper development of the infant will be undertaken on a routine basis. Prenatal surgery will, in fact, be considered a medical speciality by the year 2000.

A REAL CHANCE FOR AN AIDS VACCINE

The worldwide scourge of Acquired Immune Deficiency Syndrome has had a special impact on California. An estimated 1.5 million Americans are infected with HIV, the AIDS virus, and a disproportionate share, probably 20 percent of the infected, live in California. This means that in the state there are probably 300,000 citizens carrying the virus. To date, some 25,000 have died.[13] By 1991, the AIDS deaths in San Francisco alone (7,500) represented more than 1 percent of the entire population of the city. The HIV infection brings at least an 80 percent chance of developing AIDS over the next decade. If the estimates of present HIV infection are accurate, this means that at least 200,000 Californians will develop AIDS by the year 2000; some estimates run up to half a million.

There is no known cure for the disease, and at the present time it is 100 percent fatal. By the year 2000, treatment for the disease will be much more effective than it is at the present time, and a whole pharmacology of new and improved drugs will be available to postpone the effects of the disease. The average anticipated life span of an AIDS patient from the time of onslaught is now about ten years.

It is likely that by the end of the decade, the life span of a new AIDS sufferer will be fifteen to thirty years, depending on how early the disease is detected and how professional a program the patient is following. It may even become possible to arrest or so retard damage by the virus that an AIDS sufferer can live out a relatively normal life span.

Almost certainly, there will be an effective vaccine for AIDS by the year 2000.

Vaccines are not easily developed. There is still no vaccine for the viruses that cause chicken pox, malaria, or even the common cold. Considering that HIV was not even identified until 1985, work on the HIV vaccine is moving ahead at a remarkable clip. The consensus among leading researchers and experts is that a vaccine is eminently doable. The search for an AIDS vaccine is especially frustrating because an immunization has never before been developed against a "retrovirus," the class of viruses discovered just a decade ago. These "retroviruses" can insinuate their own genetic material into the cells they infect. Nevertheless, current optimism stems from preliminary studies both in animals and in humans. At the present time, there are six candidate vaccines, all in the early stage of testing. One is a genetically engineered combination of a protein and carbohydrate termed a glycoprotein. This vaccine is now undergoing limited testing on sixty men and women not infected with the virus. If they have no negative side-effects from the vaccine and no unwanted reactions, doses will be increased so that doctors can determine whether they can trigger the immune systems of the volunteers to mobilize antibodies. Because the AIDS virus comes in many different strains and tends to mutate frequently, it is expected that a really successful AIDS vaccine will be a "cocktail" made up of a number of different viral proteins.

Large-scale testing of an AIDS vaccine will certainly be in operation by the year 1996, and a safe and effective vaccine will be in general use by the year 2000. The AIDS vaccine will definitely precede any AIDS "cure," if in fact a cure is ever discovered. More likely, "holding action" drugs will be in general use long before any cure for the AIDS scourge is available.

SOLVING THE PROBLEM OF THE MEDICALLY UNINSURED

The amount that Americans spend on health insurance premiums rose on the average more than 12 percent each year during the past decade. The total cost increased from $55 billion to an astonishing $175 billion. For Californians, the effects of the increased cost of insurance were devastating. California's population increased by 17 percent over that period, but the ranks of the uninsured increased by 46 percent.[14] At last count, there were over 5.5 million Californians without health insurance of any kind, almost one-quarter of the working-age population of the state.

One problem, of course, is the sheer cost of health insurance and of health care in the country. Per-capita health spending in the United States is in excess of $2,500 a year, almost twice that of most countries in the industrialized world.[15] Another problem is the trend in insurance to exclude the sick. High blood pressure, high blood sugar, overweight, past substance abuse, or any chronic health problem will ordinarily exclude a Californian from a private health plan. The growing number of uninsured Californians will undoubtedly necessitate some solution before the year 2000. In all probability, one or a combination of the following programs will be in place by the end of the decade.

Mandatory Workplace Insurance. Companies with a minimum number of employees would be required to offer health insurance to their workers as a company or shared expense, or the companies would be required to pay into a state fund that would provide insurance for those who can't get it through their jobs. To hold down the rates, the state would regulate rates of physicians and hospitals.

Hospital Group Insurance. Insurers, in concert with the hospital industry in the state, would offer health insurance to individuals and groups, but without state regulation of costs. Instead, insurance companies would negotiate budgets with hospitals and doctors for the care of the insured group. If hospital and doctor fees exceed the negotiated budget, the medical institutions would take the loss.

Extended Medicaid. Federal medical coverage such as the present Medicaid would be extended to everyone with incomes below the poverty level, and employers would be required to insure their workers. There would be no regulation of fees or prices.

The California State Health Access Plan. Private insurance would be eliminated. The state would fund a single plan for all Californians, much like the Canadian plan. The state would pay for all health-care costs and tax the population of the state to cover costs. Medical rates would be set by a state board.

California Medical Association Health System. State hospitals, doctors, and insurers would organize into large health plans, which would then sell health-care insurance to businesses and to the state itself for the unemployed and poor. All employees would pay a monthly premium, and the health plans would negotiate rates with the businesses of the state. There would be no regulation of medical charges outside of the negotiation. No competitive insurance plans would be offered in the state.

It is very likely that one or both of these last two state plans will be offered as a state initiative on the ballot before 1994 and could be in full effect by the end of the year 2000.

BY THE YEAR 2000:

It is almost certain that:

- Health costs for the average Californian will have more than doubled over the previous decade.
- Infant mortality in California will be at an all-time low.
- The life span of the average Californian will be several years longer than it is today.
- California will have more than 90,000 doctors and 20,000 dentists practicing in the state.

- There will be as many as 2,000 nursing homes for the elderly in the state.
- Less than one-fourth of all adults in California will still be regular smokers.
- The average registered nurse working in the state will make more than $80,000 a year.

It is very likely that:

- There will be a vaccine for Acquired Immune Deficiency Syndrome.
- Health care will reach 15 percent of the state's gross product.
- California will have the lowest overall cancer rates of any state in the union.
- Half of all the hospitals currently operating in California will be closed or merged.
- There will be a limit on California jury awards for pain and suffering in medical malpractice suits.
- A quarter of a million Californians will live in nursing homes.
- Gene therapy will replace chemotherapy as treatment for a number of forms of cancer.
- It will cost about $1,500 a day to stay in a California hospital.
- Antitrust laws will be suspended to allow negotiations between California health-care providers and consumers to develop prices and payment rates.
- There will be a new $175 million Veterans Administration Hospital in the Davis/Sacramento area.
- Some babies born in California will have mothers who are in their late fifties.

It is even possible that:

- There will be a cure for AIDS.
- All employees of California companies with more than ten workers will be covered by health insurance.
- Brain surgery on blocked arteries to prevent strokes will be commonplace.

- Both nearsightedness and farsightedness will be cured by simple laser treatments in the doctor's office.
- There will be an effective treatment to halt the onslaught of Alzheimer's disease.
- Safe and effective vaccines will be developed for chicken pox, malaria, genital herpes, and the common cold.
- As a result of pressure from Medicare, most routine surgeries will be cheaper than they are now.
- The abortion pill RU-486 will be in general use in California.
- The average Californian born in the year 2000 will live ten years longer than the average Californian dying in that year.

California and the Environment

The great struggle of the 1980s between the advocates of California growth and development versus those wishing to preserve and protect the California environment will continue to be the great struggle of the 1990s.

With as many as 5 million more people coming to California, there will be a real need for more homes, more industry, more roads, more malls, more jobs, more cars. But what will the cost be in terms of greater air and water pollution, fewer forests and open land areas, increased toxics and pollutants? How much more development can the state endure without seriously damaging its natural beauty? How crowded can California become without compromising the way of life that attracted so many people to come to the state in the first place?

THE QUEST FOR CLEAN AIR

Parts of California, like all of the world's industrialized areas, have a serious problem with air pollution. The number of days in California with unhealthful air (ozone concentration of 12 parts per million for at least one hour) varies from 0 in Yolo County to 165 in Los Angeles County. Ten counties in the state have more than 50 such days in an average year, roughly one day out of every week.[1] The resulting damage to the lungs of a large portion of the state's population is considerable. The damage to farm crops is becoming more apparent with each passing season. Fortunately, help is on the way at three different levels, and this three-pronged attack will make a considerable difference over the remainder of the decade.

Federal: The National Clean Air Act of 1990 requires utilities to cut their annual sulfur dioxide emissions to half the current levels by the year 2000 either by installing "scrubbers" or by using low-sulfur coal. Industry must reduce emissions of 189 toxic chemicals by 90 percent over the decade. Auto pollution, the chief cause of smog, must be cut by 60 percent by 1998. Oil companies must offer cleaner-burning fuel, such as a gasoline-ethanol blend, by 1995 in Los Angeles. The use of CVCs and other fluorocarbons must be reduced by 20 percent by 1993 and 50 percent by 1998.[2]

State: The California Air Resources Board has ordered reductions in the amount of smog-forming hydrocarbons emitted from hair sprays, air fresheners, glass cleaners, and thirteen other common household products. These new regulations will take effect between 1993 and 1998, and they are expected to reduce such emissions in California by an estimated 45 tons per day.[3] The board has also adopted a plan to reduce pollution from automobiles by 50 to 80 percent within the decade. Since the beginning of 1992, it has been illegal to sell leaded gasoline at California service stations. Starting in 1994, automobile makers must begin introducing models that emit no more than half the amount of hydrocarbons emitted at present. By 1998, 2 percent of all the automobiles sold in the state must have zero emissions, meaning they must be electric cars. By 2003, 10 percent of all new cars must have zero emissions, and the remainder must not exceed emissions 70 percent below 1993 standards.[4]

Regional: Regulatory bodies, such as the South Coast Air Quality Management District in Southern California, are making their own regulations to deal with their own specific air pollution problems. AQMD, in addition to making specific regulations for industries, utilities, and consumers in its own area, has budgeted $6.82 million in matching funds to finance private industry research into better and cheaper ways to control smog. These means of smog control will range from low-pollution heaters to clean-burning methanol diesel buses.[5] The Bay Area Air Quality Management District is promulgating its own regulations to reduce car emissions, promote mass transit, and place tighter pollution controls on local industry.

By the year 2000, air quality in almost all parts of California will be dramatically improved, with days of unhealthful air (the 12 ppm standard) cut in half. The biggest change will be in the Southern California area, where, as one authority has stated, "You're going to see air that by L.A. standards is unbelievably good, even before the turn of the century."[6]

THE REDWOODS WILL STAND

Perhaps the most dramatic point of conflict between business interests and environmentalists concerns California's remaining stands of old-growth redwood forests. While most of these ancient redwoods are now under governmental jurisdiction of some kind, others remain in private hands. One of the largest stands of California ancient redwoods still privately owned is in the Headwaters Forest in Northern California. The Headwaters Forest is a basic test case as to whether additional logging of the forests will be permitted in the state in the 1990s.

Two initiatives, Propositions 128 and 130, which would have authorized bonds for the purchase of the Headwaters Forest, were recently rejected by the voters. Now the Board of Forestry is considering an appeal from the owners of this forest to permit logging in two parcels of this 3,000-acre forest in Humboldt County. The environmental community, supported now by Governor Pete Wilson, has urged the board to turn down the request. This makes the governor's position clear: he will work with environmental groups to preserve old growth. As one of his principal assistants stated, "We need to work together to preserve old-growth redwood stands. He is going to look for a responsible and equitable plan to make that happen."[7]

The working alliance between the governor's office and responsible environmental organizations will endure through the governor's time in office, which should mean through most of the decade of the 1990s.

There are an estimated 75,000 acres of old-growth redwoods left in California.[8] In the year 2000, at least 95 percent of these historic trees will still be standing, with cutting all but eliminated except in a few remote areas. California's celebrated redwood forests will be around for local admirers and tourists to enjoy at the end of this century and at the end of the following century.

A more challenging long-range danger to California's forests is air pollution. There are approximately 33 million acres of various kinds of forests in the state, covering one-third of the state's land surface. There is evidence that air pollution is damaging these trees in a number of areas in the state. Ozone damage has been found in the forests of Southern California and in the southern and mid-range Sierra Nevada. In all, 50 percent of the forested areas in 12 counties and 5 out of 19 national forests have been found to be at risk from air pollution.[9]

This condition will be somewhat improved by the year 2000 as a result of more rigid regulations and more stringent enforcement of pollution standards, but some risk to California forests from air pollution will continue into the twenty-first century.

CLEANING UP CALIFORNIA'S SHORES AND WATERWAYS

Almost 300 waterways in California are seriously polluted, 17 by toxic waste from industrial plants or sewage treatment plants.[10] The ocean floor of the Gulf of the Farallones, off the coast of San Francisco, has recently been discovered to be littered with corroded, collapsed drums of radioactive waste over a 30-mile area.[11] Vast areas of California's shoreline, victimized by military, commercial, and civic dumping, show serious signs of pollution.

The future for California's water areas, however, is far from bleak. New laws, more stringent regulations, and an aroused citizenry will combine to halt further serious damage and even to reverse the mistreatment of California's rivers, lakes, shores, and wetlands.

The State Water Resources Control Board is cracking down on waste discharges by industry and by municipalities. Time limits will be established and financial penalties exacted.

The Supreme Court has determined that cities and counties in California have the right to pass laws impeding drilling off their shores and to regulate their own harbors and ocean resources.

The state government will pass bills to provide the strongest protection yet to preserve California's coastline. They will ban all future oil drilling in state-controlled waters and will create a sanctuary along the entire coast three miles out. After the year 2005, no sewage will be dumped into the ocean unless bacteria and pollutants have been removed from it.

International agreements among the world's largest nations will result in global banning of the dumping of industrial waste at sea. Forty-three nations will be signatories to the London Dumping Convention, which will phase out all such industrial waste disposal by the year 1995.

California business and industry will spend billions of dollars in the 1990s to reduce their own water pollution, to recycle discharged water for secondary use, and to create new systems to prevent dangerous runoff. A whole new technology for treating sewage and urban runoff will be developed.

By the year 2000, the shores and waterways of California will be less polluted than they are today. The state's wetlands will be largely preserved. There will be no additional oil drilling in California's three-mile coastal area in the Pacific.

ALTERNATIVE AGRICULTURE—FOOD WITHOUT CHEMICALS

Ten percent of all the pesticides used in the world are used in California, as are almost half of all the pesticides used in the United States.[12] California agriculture is, of course, the dominant user of these pesticides on a wide variety of crops from corn to grapes to fruit trees. The most widely used chemicals are chlorine, sulfur, and petroleum products, but dozens of other major pesticides are also used regularly in California fields.[13]

Californians have at least three concerns about such widespread use of these chemicals. The first is their possible ingestion of these pesticides with the fruits and vegetables they consume. The second is the danger they present to those working with these chemicals in the fields. The third is the impact that pesticides and fertilizers have on California's underground and surface water supply. Half of all wells in the state, for instance, are contaminated with nitrates, while pesticides have been found not only in surface water but in rain and fog as well. As a consequence, farmers and environmentalists, as well as university and governmental agriculturists, are eager to reduce the use of chemicals wherever possible. Part of the job is being done by the federal government, which bans certain kinds of chemicals. Beyond this, even the use of permissible chemicals is gradually declining. The trend toward alternative or organic farming in California is clear.

Genetic engineering is already producing biological pest controls that will replace many of the chemicals used today. Currently, researchers, in two separate experiments, have produced toxin-producing genes from mites and scorpions and inserted them in viruses that kill insect pests. The toxins paralyze the insects and prevent them from eating vegetation even before it kills them.[14] This technique makes it possible to create efficient, genetically engineered viruses aimed at a single pest. It is also expected that insects are unlikely to develop immunity to these new genetic weapons.

The bulk of agricultural research in California is done by University of California experts at Davis, Berkeley, and Riverside. They are making experiments and concepts in non- and reduced-chemical agriculture available to state farmers in ever-increasing numbers. Farmers will soon be able to reduce dramatically their dependency on chemicals. Corn, for instance, is now the largest single user of pesticides in California, and it may be possible to cut the use of pesticides and chemicals for corn by as much as 80 percent. There could also be a cut of 50 percent in use by the state's citrus industry, 35 percent in the state's grape industry, and 30 percent in alfalfa.

No matter what the eventual degree of decline, there is no doubt that the trend toward the reduced use of chemicals in California agriculture is unstoppable. By the year 2000, a large percentage of California's best-known crops will be grown organically and almost all California produce will be brought to

market with far lower use of chemicals and pesticides than at the
present time.

URBAN TRASH INTO COMPOST

California, along with the rest of the United States, produces trash
at a rate unmatched anywhere in the world. The average Californian
throws away four pounds of garbage a day, and that figure is on the
rise.[15] This overload of refuse presents both an environmental and
economic problem to the state. Collecting and disposing of this daily
mountain of garbage represents a major expenditure as well as a
major civic problem. California's existing landfills are rapidly filling
up, and many of them will be out of business by the end of the
decade. The "not in my backyard" syndrome, plus increasingly
stringent environmental regulations, makes the creation of new
landfills extremely difficult. Most local efforts at reducing trash have
lost money or have been bogged down by citizen apathy. The
solution: commercial composting. Composting plants can be built
that transform household and business waste into useful, safe
compost, using high-tech versions of the natural process that turns
organic matter into loam. The resulting residue can then be used for
topsoil for filling around building sites, for covering highway
medians, and even for sealing landfills themselves.

The Solid Waste Composting Council, a consortium of compost
equipment makers, waste-management firms, and consumer goods
makers, will begin a program of helping local governments to set up
composting programs in their own communities. The plan will offer
cities and regional governments information on composting technology, a clearing house on regulatory law, market-application
studies, technical evaluations, and on-site tours of the fourteen
operating municipal trash-composting facilities that already exist in
the country. The technology is moving so fast that within a single
year, 1991, these facilities increased from 14 to 24.[16]

**The campaign to turn urban trash into usable compost will be
fought by some environmentalists who prefer a greater emphasis
on recycling, but composting is a science whose time has come,
and the advantages of building major composting plants is**

persuasive. By the year 2000, most large local governments in California with landfill problems will turn to composting as the logical and inevitable answer to the growing mountains of urban trash.

A NEW SOLUTION TO NUCLEAR WASTE

California generates an estimated 90,000 cubic feet of low-level nuclear waste every year, more than any other state.[17] A site in the Mojave Desert near Needles has been selected for the storage of low-level nuclear waste from both California and Arizona. Once it is activated, it will be the state's major depository for at least a decade.

However, the long-range solution to the problem of disposing of atomic waste may not be storage but a process called "transmutation." Now only a theory, "transmutation" could be operational within a decade or so. In time, it could solve the problem of what to do with the world's annual supply of radioactive waste, enough to fill a cube 100 feet on each side. Here's how "transmutation" would work: radioactive waste would be placed inside a particle accelerator. The accelerator then would fire protons at a "target" that, in turn, emits neutrons at the waste. The neutrons would be absorbed into the waste's atomic nuclei or otherwise alter the nucleic structure, which, in turn, would transform the atoms into different elements. Through this process, the waste would become either less radioactive or entirely nonradioactive.[18]

Transmutation has the potential to destroy nuclear waste more completely and efficiently than any other system yet imagined. It also poses little or no danger to those involved in handling the materials or supervising the process.

It is unlikely that the system of transmutation will be operational by the year 2000, but it could be available within a short time after the turn of the century. It is possible that by that time the process could be so refined that it could turn radioactive atomic waste into a precious metal called "Ruthenium," which could be sold commercially.

MANURE AND PAINT—AN UNUSUAL SOLUTION

Soon it may become possible to transform hazardous wastewater created by the printing and paint industries by an unusual treatment called "biodegradation."[19] Biodegradation uses the waste product of horses to break down water-based paints and inks. Naturally occurring microbes present in horse manure are the working ingredient that can turn this kind of toxic water into reusable water or into a clay-like solid that can be used to make plastics or cement.

This remarkable process, using a "secret ingredient" that is in ready supply on many California farms, promises a simple and natural solution to a complex environmental problem. These kinds of hazardous waste water are now treated and discharged into California's sewers or dumped into the state's landfills. By the turn of the century, water polluted by print and paint residue will be "biodegraded" and restored to a safe and useful form.

THE END OF BURNING RICE

One-quarter of all the rice grown in the United States and 2 percent of all the rice grown in the world is grown in an 11-county area just north of California's capital. The production of this fine product, however, does not come without a price. Every year the industry creates a serious problem of pollution when farmers burn the 1.2 million tons of rice straw left in the fields after harvest.[20] Environmentalists have argued for decades that straw burning has been a major factor in fouling California's air and injuring people with allergies and lung ailments. With a rapidly growing urban population of over a million, Sacramento and its rice-growing neighbors have been eager to find a solution to this environmental problem.

By the end of the decade, the solution will be in place. When the new century arrives, the rice industry will have essentially phased out the practice of burning rice straw in the autumn. Burning will be permitted only on a limited number of acres if there is proof of stem-rot to the rice plants. This understanding,

arrived at in discussions between rice growers, environmentalists, and legislators is now formulated into law. The ban will commence in the year 2000.

NEW AND BETTER PARKS FOR CALIFORNIA

More than one-quarter of the land surface of California is under the protection of the state and federal park systems. National forests cover 20 percent of the state, national parks 5 percent, and state parks 1 percent. Another .5 percent is made up of city parks and recreation areas.

There are, of course, problems in California's parks, just as there are in parks across the nation. Some are victims of shoddy management. Exotic species sometimes endanger native wildlife. Miners mine—both legally and illegally. Poachers kill legally protected animals for profit. But the biggest problem with California parks is that they are crowded. Every year, some 80 million people come to California's state parks, and more than 40 million visit the seven national parks in California.[22]

As many as 30,000 people often descend on Yosemite Valley on a single summer day.[23] The resulting crowding and pollution are a legitimate cause for concern by park officials. With California's parks stretched to the breaking point, it comes as welcome news that Congress has approved the biggest sum for park acquisition in a decade. A total of $343 million has been appropriated for acquisition, and $39 million, more than 10 percent of the total, will be spent in California.[24]

Here is a short list of some of the new parklands that will be purchased in the remainder of the decade and converted to parks:

In Northern California: a 140-acre site next to John Muir Woods, ranchland west of the Napa River, Castle Peak on the Pacific Crest Trail, the North Ford of the American River, the King Range Conservation Area, the Lake Tahoe Basin, the Sacramento River National Wildlife Refuge Area.

In Central California: the Los Padres National Forest, the South Fork of the Merced River, the Carrizo Plains, the Toiyabe National Forest's Hope Valley.

In Southern California: the East Mojave National Scenic Area, the Desert Tortoise Natural Area, an area of the Chuckwalla Bench.

In addition to these new national parks, the state itself will establish additional park areas, including the creation of "greenways" along many of California's finest rivers. There will be 31 such greenways, including belts along the Petaluma and Russian rivers, the San Rafael Canal, the Laguna de Santa Rosa in Sebastopol, and Coyote Creek in Santa Clara and San Jose counties.[25]

By the year 2000, both the national and state parks will be considerably expanded, adding another 2 percent of California's land surface to the systems. To alleviate overcrowding, some existing major parks, among them Yosemite National Park, will accept visitors on a reservations-only basis. Entrance fees at most parks will be more than double their present cost.

ANIMALS OR PEOPLE: THE COMING STRUGGLE BETWEEN THE SPECIES

Probably no single tool of the environmentalists has created as much controversy or bitterness as their use of the Endangered Species Act, a piece of federal legislation that protects animals and animal forms that are threatened with extinction. This legislation provides one of the few hooks that give conservationists legal standing in their effort to prevent change and to preserve forests and waterways in their current condition. In essence, these threatened creatures, sometimes virtually unknown species, become surrogates for issues that are basic to the well-being and even the survival of many Californians.

In the forests of the Northwest, the spotted owl, previously unheralded in its importance to the ecological balance of the planet, has become the surrogate in the battle between those wishing to conserve old-growth forests versus those holding jobs in the lumber industry. The previously unrecognized snail darter has been made the stand-in for a confrontation on a badly needed dam. Recently, the proposed Los Baños Grande reservoir, a project that would provide 2 million acre-feet of water annually to thirsty Californians, was effectively killed because it would, among other things, endanger a habitat of the San Joaquin kit fox.

Now a three-inch fish that smells like a cucumber and lives only in the Sacramento River delta is being used as the point of contention that may keep water in the area from being shipped to farms and cities in California. Thus the delta smelt, a fish of no known use, could keep a vital water source from the thirsty urban masses and from farmers already desperate for water for irrigation.

What is happening, of course, is that the Endangered Species Act is being used to pit the well-being of certain animal species against the well-being of certain human beings. It juxtaposes two opposing views of what is good for the planet and what is important to society. This struggle will become more intense in California in the final years of the decade. During this decade, more and more cases will arise in which the interests of certain groups of Californians will be weighed against those of other forms of animal life. In reality, these struggles will be contests between those who believe in economic expansion and those whose concerns are largely environmental.

By the year 2000, there will be less tolerance for the narrow-mindedness of some environmental legislation, including the Endangered Species Act. The courts will act to restrict use of this law for purposes that are detrimental to important segments of human society.

DROUGHTS TAKE THEIR TOLL

A prolonged drought can take a serious toll on the California environment. The recent study of the five-year dry spell indicates that it has caused severe damage to a wide variety of environmental elements.[26]

Large areas of valuable trees in the Sierra Nevada died from lack of water and from resulting pest infestations. The population of water fowl declined as wetland habitats shrank or deteriorated. The winter-run chinook salmon was dramatically reduced in numbers because of low river flows. The number of coho and chinook salmon off the coast plummeted. The number of striped bass in the Sacramento Delta dropped dramatically. The herring industry in Tomales Bay,

north of San Francisco, has been virtually destroyed because the
reduced flow of fresh water made the bay too saline.

There was also a massive loss of hydroelectric power, which
dropped from 20 percent to 12 percent of the state's total electric
power. This drop, in turn, meant that utilities had to replace the
decline in hydroelectric power by burning fossil fuels at additional
economic cost and increased air pollution.

This drought should end soon, as cyclical climatic changes take
place, and many of these environmental conditions will be restored.
But there will probably be another drought before or around the year
2000. If drought strikes again, it will wreak its toll on the animal and
plant life of California once again.

THE ATTEMPT TO TAME GROWTH THROUGH REGIONAL PLANNING

Many environmental experts feel that the greatest threat to the
future of California ecology is the sheer numbers of people
descending on the state. At the present rate of 5 to 6 million
additional residents every decade, California's land, water, and skies
come under a growing threat of simply being overrun. No mecha-
nism is available to keep people from coming to California in such
numbers. Immigration laws are federally controlled and out of the
state's hands, and it is illegal, of course, to close California's borders
or even make entry to the state difficult. Only a few factors might
slow down California's future growth:

A shortage of jobs. The forecast is that the state's economy will
generate 3 million new jobs in the 1990s, but if this increase does not
materialize and jobs are hard to come by in the state, it could
discourage migration at the predicted level.

The high cost of housing. The cost of buying or renting a
residence in California is already far beyond the national norms. If
the differential between living in California and living elsewhere
continues to expand, it could dampen the enthusiasm of Americans
from other states for moving to California.

The destruction of the "California life-style." If California's
problems of overcrowding, crime, urban sprawl, and a deteriorating

environment continue to erode the charm of living in the state, the attraction of coming to California could wane.

Taxes. California is on its way to having the highest income taxes and the highest sales taxes in the country. If this trend continues, the financial penalty for coming to California could prove punitive for prospective newcomers.

A lack of jobs, however, did not keep Americans from trekking to California during the Depression. The high cost of buying a home and of establishing residence in California has not yet noticeably reduced the ardor of the California-bound. The daily problems that people face when they come here to live probably seem no greater than those they left behind. Just one other workable solution is apparent: local and regional planning.

A growing number of local entities have taken it on themselves, usually through public referenda, to limit the growth of their municipalities. For instance, voters in Half Moon Bay, which is south of San Francisco, recently voted overwhelmingly to limit population growth in the city to 3 percent per year, which translates to about 100 new housing units a year.[27] Other cities, including Walnut Creek, have passed ordinances limiting the height and size of new buildings. These local ordinances will scarcely stanch the rush to California, however. Passing such measures is a little like squeezing a balloon; apply pressure in one spot and it simply bulges out somewhere else.

Planning by regional government is the latest proposed panacea. A gleam in planners' eyes for over three decades, regional government is seen by many as the brightest hope for limiting the state's growth. Regional planning envisions placing a cross section of interests—transportation, air and water quality, mass transit, waste disposal, open land management—in the hands of regional governments that would ignore city and county lines. One such bill introduced in Sacramento would create a governmental unit that would combine and blend agencies from seven urban regions in the San Francisco Bay Area to supervise all long-range planning and to impose restrictions on the area's relentless growth.

It is unlikely, however, that regional government will make any serious headway in this decade, particularly in regard to

land-use planning. The principal inhibitor of regional government will be the jealously guarded prerogatives of politically
powerful local officials. It will be well after the year 2000 before
any substantive regional governmental bodies take shape. In the
meantime, there will be no viable means of slowing the spiraling
growth of the state of California.

LEARNING TO LIVE WITH TOXIC WASTE

A sad truth is beginning to dawn on many scientists and experts
concerned with California's environment: the cost of cleaning up all
of the state's polluted sites and areas is probably prohibitive, and the
money that would have to be allocated for that purpose can probably
be spent more wisely on other environmental situations. Of the some
10,000 toxic sites identified nationwide by Superfund authorities,
2,826 are in California.[28] There are 31 sites in the Bay Area alone,
most of them in Silicon Valley in Santa Clara County. Costs of a total
cleanup of all sites in the country are now projected to be in excess
of $1 trillion, and they could be considerably higher than that.[29] The
likelihood, therefore, of all of the California sites being completely
cleaned up is extremely slim.

Most current legislation requires a standard of cleanup that is
probably unattainable at any price. Regulations tend to mandate
"permanent remedies" rather than compromise measures that could
ensure basic protection of public health. For instance, a requirement
that groundwater be returned to "utterly pristine condition" is
probably beyond the ability of current technology and would require
an effort extending over several centuries.

By the start of the next century, authorities, regulators, and
legislators will admit that, generally speaking, it is not economically feasible to clean up all toxic wastes in California.

The economic cost of carrying out a total and complete program
will be deemed to be far greater than any benefit in human health
that it can generate. The toxic clean-up campaign necessarily will be
compromised, and the public will have to learn to live with at least
some level of toxic pollution.

THE EARTHQUAKE FACTOR—COULD CALIFORNIA
LOSE IT ALL?

Living with earthquakes is a way of life for Californians. Over the last century and a half, there have been quakes of sufficient magnitude to bring life in parts of the state to a virtual halt.

The San Andreas Fault, running from north of San Francisco to south of Los Angeles, has given California its biggest shakes: an estimated 8.3 in 1906 in San Francisco and an estimated 8.0 in 1857 in Fort Tejon. More recently, it shook most of the San Francisco Bay Area with a 7.1 jolt in 1989.

The Hayward Fault, running along the eastern edge of San Francisco Bay, shook Fremont with an estimated 7.0 jolt in 1868; it hammered Oakland with another 7.0 shock in 1936.[31]

The question, of course, is whether or not California has an earthquake in its future that will seriously damage the state's ecology, as well as its economy. All that scientists can do is quote the odds. One study, released in July of 1990 by the United States Geological Survey, estimates a 67 percent chance of another earthquake the size of the 1989 quake during the next thirty years; it states also that the quake could hit at any time.[32] This 1990 study increased the odds over a 1988 USGS estimate of a 50 percent chance of such a quake in thirty years (and one happened a year later, of course).

The USGS further estimates the following odds on a 7.0 quake in these areas in the next three decades: Hayward Fault, northern section (28 percent); Hayward Fault, southern section (23 percent); San Andreas Fault, southern section (23 percent); Rodgers Creek Fault, Sonoma County (22 percent).

If the Bay Area were to have a 7.5-magnitude quake, it is estimated that there would be up to 4,500 fatalities, 135,000 injuries, and $40 billion in damage.[33] No odds are given on a quake of that dimension.

It can be said, then, that the odds are only about 1 out of 5 that another quake of sufficient intensity to cause serious human and environmental damage will hit California by the year 2000. By the year 2020, the odds will increase to 2 out of 3.

THE CHANGING MYTHOLOGY OF ENVIRONMENTALISM

For years, California's environmentalists have been guided by certain articles of faith. By the start of the next century, a number of these tenets of environmentalism will be in retreat.

Paper is better than plastic. Environmentalists have probably carried plastic-bashing too far. Plastic products, including throwaway foam plastic cups, have been portrayed as villains for choking landfills with nonbiodegradable material, for consuming nonrenewable resources, and for releasing gases that endanger the ozone layer. Recent discoveries indicate, however, that paper actually uses up more raw materials, including petroleum, requires more energy for steam and machinery, dumps more pollution into water supplies, takes up more space in landfills, and is more likely to pollute landfills.

Polystyrenes help deplete the ozone layer. Until recently, most polystyrene products were made with chlorofluorocarbons (CFCs), which deplete the ozone layer. Now, however, most manufacturers have switched to CFC substitutes, which either destroy ozone at a dramatically reduced rate or do not destroy ozone at all.

Biodegradability is good. There is a growing suspicion in scientific circles that degradability in recycling and incinerating is irrelevant. Garbage, it is now believed by many, does not actually break down in landfills, and it may actually be harmful because it can release toxic substances into the atmosphere and into the environment.

In this decade, increasingly sophisticated studies that follow products from factory to dump will cast new light and new suspicions on long-held environmental convictions that have become more emotional than logical. The sacred text of environmentalism will undergo considerable revision by the year 2000.

A NEW SUPERAGENCY WATCHDOG FOR THE ENVIRONMENT

The newly created California Environmental Protection Agency will oversee almost all aspects of the state's environment by the year

2000. Included under its jurisdiction will be the Air Resources Board, the Water Resources Control Board, the Integrated Waste Management Board, a new Department of Toxic Substance Control, an Office of Pollution Prevention, and an Office of Regulations and Standards.

The department will have broad powers to protect the environmental well-being of California. It will have powers to make regulations in certain areas, to recommend legislation, and to see that laws concerning the environment are adequately enforced.

The activities of this superagency watchdog will be overseen by a Secretary of Environmental Protection who will be appointed by the governor. The agency will have general jurisdiction over air quality, water purity, waste disposal, the use of toxic chemicals, atomic waste, and standards of safety in agricultural and food products.

By the year 2000, this new California Environmental Protection Agency will be a powerful force in maintaining and preserving the beauty, the safety, and the enjoyment of life in California, and it will be the focal point in the struggle between the state's expansionists and environmentalists.

BY THE YEAR 2000:

It is almost certain that:

- California's air quality will be considerably improved.
- The use of chemicals in California agriculture will be reduced by at least 50 percent.
- Real regional planning will still be in the future.
- Car emissions in the state will be reduced by at least 40 percent.
- There will be no more burning of rice straw in California.
- Sulfur-dioxide emissions into California air from industry will be reduced by one-half, nitrogen oxides by one-third.
- Another 1 percent of California's land surface will be developed. Still another 2 percent will become parkland.
- Californians will be bravely anticipating another major earthquake in the 7.0 range.

It is very likely that:

- The number of unhealthful air days in California will be cut in half.
- The Endangered Species Act will be hemmed in by the courts to prevent it from inflicting extreme hardships on specific groups of Californians.
- About 20 percent of all fruits and vegetables sold in California will be organically grown.
- There will be a new $40 million experimental solar energy plant in the Mojave Desert generating power with giant mirrors and molten salt.
- The most popularly used gasolines will emit 35 percent fewer pollutants into the air.
- The new California Environmental Agency will be given sweeping powers to oversee the well-being of the state's environment.
- California will not have another earthquake of 7.0 magnitude.

It is even possible that:

- Paper will become a bigger environmental villain than plastic.
- More than 5 million more acres of desert in southeastern California will be placed under federal jurisdiction.
- The problem of nuclear waste will be largely under control, thanks to exotic new treatments.
- Yosemite National Park will be booked an average of six months in advance.
- Various species of rats and mice will be added to the list of endangered species.
- California will have an earthquake greater than 7.0.

10

Crime and Criminals in California

California is the seventh most violent state in the nation.[1] Crime in the state was on the increase throughout the 1980s, with the most serious crimes of murder, burglary, robbery, and aggravated assault leading the way. As California's population increases and as it becomes less homogeneous, it is likely that the state's crime rate will continue to grow. Crime and fear for personal safety represent one of the greatest concerns of Californians in all parts of the state. Their fears are well justified.

CRIME—A CALIFORNIA GROWTH INDUSTRY

Arrests for violent crime increased by more than 30 percent in the state during the 1980s.[2] Over that same period, California's prison population increased fourfold.[3] The economic crimes of burglary, personal theft, and car theft totaled more than 7 million incidents.[4] The total dollar value of these crimes was probably in the vicinity of $20 billion.

Among California's larger cities, Richmond, Oakland, and Berkeley stand as the three most crime-ridden. Los Angeles, San Francisco, Sacramento, and San Diego also show significant increases in major crime. The three safest cities in California are Thousand Oaks, Simi Valley, and Sunnyvale, but even these cities have an increasing crime problem. The odds of a Californian being the victim of crime during the 1980s were not heartening.

It is likely that major crime will continue to grow throughout the 1990s. If the present trend continues, the threat to California

TABLE 10-1
CALIFORNIANS AS CRIME VICTIMS, 1980-1989

Murder	1 in 1015
Rape	1 in 112
Robbery	1 in 33
Assault	1 in 11
Burglary	1 in 6

Source: Author's analysis of figures available in *Crime and Delinquency in California, 1980–1989,* California Department of Justice.

citizens will be far greater than it is today. At the present rate of increase, Californians will be subjected to 5,300 murders, 15,000 forcible rapes, 125,000 robberies, and 260,000 aggravated assaults in the year 2000.

CALIFORNIA CRIME AND THE COCAINE CONNECTION

California's overall increase in crime is at least partly due to the growing and widespread use of illegal drugs in the state. In Los Angeles County alone, drug crimes accounted for 56 percent of all felony prosecutions in 1989.[6] And drug dealers and users tend to be repeat offenders. Nearly three-quarters of all drug-case defendants have prior criminal records.[7]

In 1987, the California legislature passed a law intended to stiffen the penalties for crack cocaine. It stipulated that crack dealers had to go to prison except in unusual cases. In fact, however, most drug dealers, particularly first offenders, get light sentences or no prison sentence at all. One study of 1,800 Superior Court cases found that only 3 percent of defendants convicted of selling cocaine and heroin were given maximum sentences. Of the other convicted dealers, 70 percent were granted probation after jail time that lasted only several days to several months. As one probation officer put it, ''You wonder why people deal drugs? Because nothing happens to them when they're caught.''[8]

There is, however, reason to have hope for the future and to believe that drug-related crime and casual sentencing will go through a correction in this decade. First, the use of illegal drugs is clearly on the decline. A study in 1990 by the National Institute on Drug Abuse showed that 72 percent fewer Americans use cocaine monthly than did so five years ago. The number of people trying some illegal drug in the previous year was down by 25 percent. Similarly, Americans spent about $10 billion less on illegal drugs in 1990 than in 1989, according to the Office of Drug Control Policy.[9] The one disquieting note is that even as the indications of progress against cocaine use grow, the use of heroin may be on the rise. Nevertheless, the overall trend is favorable, and there is little doubt that California will be seeing progress, along with the rest of the nation, in reducing the use of drugs through the 1990s.

The use of cocaine by California residents will drop slowly but surely for the rest of the decade, particularly among high school students and casual users. This decline will permit law enforcement to concentrate more fully and effectively on hard-core users and dealers. By the year 2000, drug dealers will more routinely receive harsher sentences and longer jail terms in response to public pressure.

GETTING AWAY WITH MURDER—AND OTHER CRIMES

Every year, Californians are subjected to an almost mind-numbing array of crimes—3,500 murders, 100,000 robberies, 12,000 forcible rapes, and 180,000 aggravated assaults. In addition to these major crimes, there are almost a million and a half arrests for misdemeanors in California every year. More than 300,000 motor cars are stolen annually in the state.[10] This avalanche of crime does not necessarily result in the removal of the criminals from society.

TABLE 10-2
CRIMES AND CONVICTIONS

Crime	Number of Crimes 1980–1989	Number Currently in Prison for This Crime
Murder	29,533	8,755
Rape	122,930	2,542
Robbery	890,711	10,474
Assault	2,738,326	12,276

Source: California Department of Corrections.

Unfortunately, a large percentage of California criminals are never arrested for their crimes, even fewer are convicted, and still fewer spend much time in jail. Only 66 percent of murderers are ever arrested, 52 percent of rapists, 15 percent of car thieves, 14 percent of burglars.[11]

Crime will probably continue to grow in California throughout the 1990s, and by the year 2000 the personal threat to California citizens by criminals will be even greater than it is today. Forecasts indicate that among the felony crimes, aggravated assault will grow the most rapidly, followed by robbery, homicide, and burglary. The fastest-growing misdemeanor offenses will be assault and battery, petty theft, and drug law violations.

At some point, of course, public opinion may force a higher level of police protection, stiffer penalties, and longer jail sentences. The public's tolerance of crime and its patience with inadequate law enforcement are not limitless, but severe actions against crime will probably not take place until well after the year 2000.

MORE CRIMINALS, MORE PRISONS

The growing number of crimes and criminal convictions in California has placed real stress on the state's prison system. California's total prison population recently passed 100,000.[12] The number of prisoners in the state has risen dramatically for the past twelve years.

The recent history of imprisonment in California has followed the national trends to some degree. During the 1960s, America's prison population declined very slightly, even though crime rates rose. Then, as crime rates rose even faster during the 1970s, the U.S. prison population rose as well. By 1975, there were 240,000 people in the country's prisons. After that, the prison population grew even more rapidly, partly because of tougher attitudes in the criminal justice system, which reflected changing societal attitudes. During the 1980s, the U.S. prison population climbed to its present count of 600,000.[13] Over these years, cultural liberalism was on the wane,

FIGURE 10-1
CALIFORNIANS IN STATE PRISONS, 1980–1991

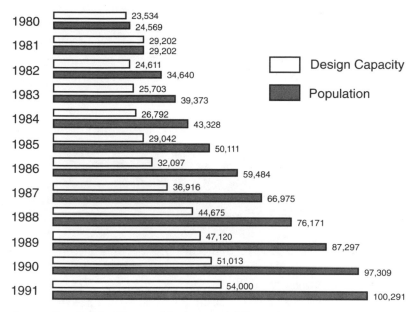

	Design Capacity	Population
1980	23,534	24,569
1981	29,202	29,202
1982	24,611	34,640
1983	25,703	39,373
1984	26,792	43,328
1985	29,042	50,111
1986	32,097	59,484
1987	36,916	66,975
1988	44,675	76,171
1989	47,120	87,297
1990	51,013	97,309
1991	54,000	100,291

Source: Los Angeles Times and Department of Corrections.

and Americans felt less collective guilt about crime and became more willing to punish individual offenders.

California, however, has now outpaced the national rate of imprisonment. At the present time, one out of every six criminals imprisoned in America is in a California prison.

Because the prison population in the state has been growing at a rate of more than 10 percent annually, overcrowding has become a serious problem in California prisons, and the construction of new prisons has been a state priority. In the 1980s, $3.3 billion—more than 14 times the cost of running the city of Oakland for a year—has been spent on eight new prisons and eight major expansions.[14] There are now twenty major prison institutions in California, including the huge, high-security institution at Pelican Bay near the Oregon border. Outside Chowchilla in the Central Valley, California also now has the world's largest prison for women.

The program of early parole in California does not seem to be the best answer to overcrowding. California has the highest rate of recidivism in the United States: 53 percent of all paroled first-time offenders are back in prison after one year, 64 percent after two years.[15] There is no reason to believe these numbers will change in the foreseeable future.

One thing is certain: the California inmate population will continue to grow. Expansion of the California prison system will continue throughout the 1990s. To operate at an acceptable level of crowding, it will be necessary to build 38 new prisons in California by the year 2000, housing 2,200 inmates each, and costing a total of $8.2 billion.[16]

The overall cost of running the California prison system will also increase dramatically. Costs escalated 372 percent between 1980 and 1989, and the budget for 1990-1991 was $2.6 billion.[17] That number will triple by the year 2000, nearing $8 billion, or 5 percent of the state budget. The cost of incarcerating a prisoner at the end of this decade could be as high as $50,000 per inmate.

At the present rate of increase, California's prison population will surpass 240,000 by the year 2000. This means that one out of every 150 Californians will be in prison at the turn of the century.

FEMALE CRIME—A GROWING PHENOMENON

The fastest-growing women's group in California, as well as in the nation, may be women behind bars. The sad truth is that, in the field of crime, women seem to be moving toward a lamentable sort of equality with men. Their share of the prison population rose more than 20 percent during the 1980s and is expected to climb even more dramatically between now and the year 2000. At present, there are over 7,100 women in California prisons, representing about 7 percent of the entire inmate population.[18]

Theft, murder, prostitution, forgery, and armed robbery are among the fastest-growing crimes committed by females in the state. But the most common crimes committed by women, as well as by men, are drug related. Almost 40 percent of California women inmates are currently imprisoned on drug convictions.[19] There are a growing number of mandatory sentencing laws which, in response to equal rights pressures, cannot discriminate by sex. As a result, judges are forced to hand out long sentences to women, some for minor or first-time offenses.

Until recently, however, women no longer found they were equal after they were locked up. They found themselves in prisons designed for, built for, and run by men. But that condition is changing and will continue to change in the years ahead.

The prototype prison for women, the Central California Women's Facility, is now in operation in Madera County. Opened in 1990, it will eventually house 2,000 female inmates. Its dormitory-style rooms incorporate many innovations in design, and communications are permitted between prisoners and with guards and officers. Each room contains four beds, a toilet, and a shower and is connected by a corridor to a core area where inmates may watch television, make phone calls, study, read, or play table games. Correctional officers will be unarmed except in a high-security cell block area, where dangerous or violent prisoners will be kept.

Crime by women will continue to grow in California throughout the 1990s, and by the year 2000 the female inmate population will at least double, reaching 15,000. At least two additional prisons expressly designed for female inmates will be built in California by the end of the century.

CRIME IN THE COUNTRYSIDE

Popular mythology envisions major crime as a big-city phenomenon. But the truth is that crime in rural California is also growing at an alarming rate. According to the Senate Judiciary Committee report, criminal violence in the rural areas is "growing at an astonishing pace" and small-town America is suffering from "skyrocketing criminal violence."[20]

This is certainly true for California, as well as many other states with large rural populations. The overall rate for violent crimes in California increased by 6.5 percent between 1989 and 1990,[21] and a good portion of this represented crime outside of what are thought of as the big-city areas. This increase is partly due to the almost pervasive use of illegal drugs today. Contrary to conventional wisdom, the drug problem is not confined to metropolitan areas, but is also ravaging small communities throughout the state.

Look for this trend to continue at least until the year 2000. Violent crime and drug-related crime will more and more become a statewide problem, not one confined to the larger cities. Crime in rural California will never reach the level of big-city violence, but the gap will continue to narrow throughout the 1990s.

RAPE—THE BRUTAL CRIME ON THE DECLINE

For reasons that are not clear, one serious crime is declining in California: rape. From 1985 to 1989, the reported forcible rapes in the state actually decreased, from 13,661 to 11,956.[22] The odds on being a victim of rape in California actually showed a 26.5 percent decrease for the decade.[23]

While the figures for 1990 show a very slight increase, they are not out of relationship with the increase in population. The surprising thing about this apparent drop in rape in California is that it defies the popular conception in the state that this crime is on the rise, a conception reinforced by recent publicity about the crime, especially on college campuses. It is also in contradiction of the national trend, which shows a rise in rape across the nation, and it is even more surprising in view of recent programs encouraging victims of rape to report the crime.

It is possible, of course, that this decade-long decline is some sort of aberration, and that the 1990s will see a resurgence of this terrible and violent crime. However, the trend has been in place for a sufficiently long time that Californians can expect that incidents of rape will not be increasing out of relationship to the

growth in California's population. By the year 2000, rape could drop yet another 5 percent as an at-risk factor for women in the state.

MINORITY CRIME IN CALIFORNIA—ON THE RISE

Crime in California is not an equal-opportunity employer. There is a great disparity in the ratio of major crime by racial group in the state, and this disparity represents one of the great challenges facing the people of California in the 1990s and into the next century. The following tables present this dilemma in dramatic fashion:

TABLE 10-3
CRIMES COMMITTED AND RACIAL GROUPS

Californians by Race		*California Felony Arrests by Race*	
White	— 57.2%	White	— 35.6%
Black	— 7.0%	Black	— 29.5%
Hispanic	— 25.8%	Hispanic	— 31.2%
Other	— 10.0%	Other	— 3.6%

Source: San Francisco Examiner and Office of the Attorney General.

For reasons that include economic deprivation, lack of self-esteem, and educational disadvantages, blacks in California commit crimes at a rate that is disproportionate to their numbers in the state's population. This is especially true when major crimes are concerned. Blacks account for 30 percent of all murders in California, as well as 33.5 percent of all rapes and 47.9 percent of all robberies.[24]

Especially tragic are the figures on California black males in the state correction system. More than 35 percent of all felons in California state prisons are black. Incredibly, one out of every three California black men between the ages of 20 and 29 is either in prison or on probation or parole.[25]

One of the great challenges facing the state for the remainder of this decade and into the twenty-first century will be to see that this incredible waste of young minority people is not permitted to continue. It is hoped that, by the year 2000, the combination of better education and increased job opportunity will make a serious dent in the amount of such crime in California.

At the start of the next century, California should more closely resemble the national statistic of one in every four young black males in the correction system. Hispanic crime will continue to rise, primarily because of the rapidly rising increase in the overall Hispanic population.

GUNS, GUNS, GUNS

The California citizenry is well-armed and is likely to remain so. To begin with, the state has almost a thousand gun clubs whose members own literally millions of weapons. It is estimated that some 2.5 million California households own more than 5 million handguns alone. Almost 4 million California households own more than 5 million rifles and 5 million shotguns. As if this were not sufficient firepower, more than 250,000 Californians own semi-automatic weapons, and more than 200 Californians have permits to own a machine-gun. Approximately one out of every three Californians—man, woman, and child—owns a gun.[26]

Recent legislation prohibits the sale of about 60 specified semi-automatic weapons in California and imposes a 15-day waiting period on those who wish to purchase any firearm. The law also requires the registration of high-powered, semi-automatic weapons in California within a certain period of time. Initially at least, this requirement was almost universally ignored; fewer than 20,000 of the estimated quarter of a million such guns were registered in the specified time.[27]

Tougher gun laws and restrictions will be in place by the year 2000, but they will not materially slow down the influx of additional weaponry into the state.

This decade will see the number of guns in California continue to grow. At present, some 30,000 licensed gun dealers in the state are selling an additional 325,000 guns to Californians every year. This means that by the year 2000, an additional 3 million guns will be at home in the state, bringing the total to almost 20 million resident firearms.

LAWYERS, LAWYERS, LAWYERS

The rising California population, the increasing complexity of California law, the state's growing crime rate, and the increasing willingness to seek satisfaction in the courts for every real or imagined injustice have all prompted a mushrooming lawyer population in the state. A 50 percent growth in the number of attorneys during the 1980s has pushed the active lawyer population in California over 100,000.[28]

There is now one lawyer for every 300 Californians. At the present rate of proliferation, there will be almost 150,000 lawyers in California by the year 2000, or one lawyer for every 240 Californians.

THE COST OF JUSTICE IN CALIFORNIA

Crime is levying a heavy burden on the taxpayers of California. The cost of California's criminal justice system has increased an average of 16 percent annually over the past decade, double the rate of growth of most state programs. Currently, justice in California has a pricetag of $10.7 billion.[29]

The cost of imprisonment alone is devastating. The state now spends more than $23,000 annually per prisoner. The total operating cost of the system is $2.6 billion.[30] When the cost of law enforcement and imprisonment is added in, the total cost of the state's criminal system is over $13 billion.

Currently, every Californian is paying an estimated $800 a year for protection against crime. By the year 2000, this figure will at least double. At the start of the twenty-first century, crime protection will come at an annual cost of over $1,500 for every California citizen.

BY THE YEAR 2000:

It is almost certain that:

• There will be 35,000 cases of arson in the state.

- The University of California at Berkeley will still have the most crime-ridden campus in America.
- 150,000 Californians will be in prison.
- The criminal justice and enforcement system in California will cost taxpayers over $20 billion.
- There will be 6 million handguns in California, as well as 9 million rifles and 6 million shotguns.
- The Supreme Court of the State of California will have at least three new members and will be considerably more conservative than it is today.
- Lethal injection will replace the gas chamber as the principal method of capital punishment.

It is very likely that:

- One out of every 25 Californians will be the victim of a violent crime during the year.
- An average of 15 California law-enforcement officers will be killed annually while on duty.
- More than a ton of explosives will be stolen in California every year.
- 15,000 California women will be in prison.
- 25,000 handguns will be stolen annually in California.
- Los Angeles will still be the bounced-check capital of the United States.
- 15,000 women in the state will be raped.
- 6,000 Californians will be murdered.

It is even possible that:

- More than 500 Californians will be on death row.
- One of every four young black California males will be in the jurisdiction of the criminal justice system.
- 500,000 Californians will have their cars stolen.
- There will be more than 150,000 active, licensed lawyers in the state.
- More than 700 prisoners will escape from California detention facilities during the year.

- There will be 85,000 public police officers in California and 130,000 private police.
- 7 million California households will own at least one firearm.
- At least 70 California lawyers will be disbarred.
- 100,000 Californians will have permits to carry a handgun.
- California will spend $50,000 incarcerating each inmate in the California prison system.
- One out of every 150 Californians will be in prison.

11

California and the Cultural Explosion

In the decade before the millennium, California and Californians will inspire a true renaissance in virtually all forms of the arts. In a search to reorder their use of leisure time and to reexamine their attitude toward life, residents of the state will pursue artistic endeavors with unprecedented zeal.

Music, theater, dance, opera, literature, and the visual arts will flourish in California as never before. The trend has been unmistakable for some time now.

- The Hollywood Bowl sold 752,000 tickets in 1990, up more than 100,000 from 1982, and is now showing a substantial profit for the first time in many years.[1]
- The San Francisco Museum of Modern Art has increased its membership from just 3,500 in the mid-seventies to more than 16,000 today.[2]
- Twenty major museums or galleries have been built in California since the mid-sixties, many of them world-celebrated for their magnificence and scope.
- San Diego's Old Globe Theater now has over 50,000 season subscribers, nearly double the membership of any other theater in the United States.[3]
- Los Angeles, according to many experts in the field, is now the most promising new art market in the world.
- Sacramento's new Central Library, just completed and due to open in 1992, will serve as a model for the nation in its literary scope, providing computerized cataloguing of books and periodicals, as

well as a vast spectrum of telecommunications and information services.

California has for decades earned a growing reputation as the new center for arts of all kinds, particularly in the field of popular culture. The state's dominance in the motion picture world has been almost absolute since the 1920s. When television became America's and the world's new phenomenon in the 1950s, Los Angeles quickly assumed the ruling position in the production of television entertainment programming. The advent of Disneyland in that same decade spawned a whole new concept in family entertainment.

Although California is better known for movie stars and rock stars, it has also been the home of some of America's greatest writers. In fact, California has, over the years, developed a literary genre that is distinctly its own—imaginative, narrative, and tough minded.

As California prospers economically, as Californians become better educated and more introspective, as new immigrants continue to bring native arts to the state, they will dramatically hasten the cultural awakening in California.

CALIFORNIANS SINGING, DANCING, ACTING, PAINTING, WRITING, SCULPTING, PLAYING, PERFORMING

The breadth and scope of cultural activities in California is truly amazing. In the professional arts, the numbers are impressive. There are more than 200 symphony orchestras in the state, and the number of smaller musical ensembles is almost beyond counting.[4] There are three full-time opera companies, as well as nineteen opera companies with shorter seasons. The California Association of Museums lists more than 250 institutions, including at least a dozen of international renown.[5]

California counts four professional ballet companies within its borders, as well as two dozen other professional dance groups. Fourteen major California theater companies are currently in operation. California boasts several dozen professional choirs and choral groups. There are more than a thousand theatrical producers and services in the state, more than 800 professional bands and orchestras, and thousands of professional registered entertainers. California is the world center for the production of motion pictures and of television shows. California has 11 percent of all the motion picture screens in the United States. As a marketplace for painting, sculpture, and the graphic arts, California ranks number one in the country. California has become a major publishing center, both of books and periodicals. Every year, more than a hundred major art festivals of various kinds are held in California cities.

The California Confederation of the Arts estimates that at the present time more than 300,000 people in California gain their livelihood in some aspect of the arts.[7] This estimate may be modest, but even so, it makes culture a major industry in the state. It means that at least one out of every one hundred Californians is making an active contribution to the cultural life of the state. And because the work and the product of these Californians are seen, heard, and enjoyed by so many others, the impact of these 300,000 is enormous.

Growth in the arts in the recent past has been impressive. Between 1960 and 1980, the work force increased 43 percent, while the number of artists, writers, and entertainers shot up by 144 percent. Then, in the 1980s, the number of such artists increased by another 80 percent, three times faster than the growth rate for all occupations.[8]

With the expected growth in the California population in this decade, and with the increasing vitality of the arts in the state, it is likely that there will be some 425,000 "California artists" by the year 2000.

ART AND ARTISTS, GALLERIES AND MUSEUMS

There are probably more than 100,000 Californians who paint, sculpt, or do graphic arts. Among them are many nationally and internationally renowned artists. To display and sell their works, as well as to show the work of artists from around the world, more than 5,000 art galleries operate within the state. Equally impressive is the number of California museums, probably more than 500 in all.[9] At least half of the museums are of sufficient importance to be members of the California Association of Museums. Among them are the Crocker Art Museum in Sacramento, the oldest public art museum in the West; the J. Paul Getty Museum in Santa Monica, housing a renowned permanent collection of Greek and Roman sculpture; the Los Angeles Municipal Art Gallery, which exhibits the works of living California artists; the Oakland Museum with its outstanding history of California art; and the Armand Hammer Museum of Art in Brentwood with its eclectic collection of European and classic artworks.

The future of California galleries and museums is bright indeed. The interest in California art is constantly growing and expanding. The number of art galleries in the state can be expected to increase by 20 percent before the turn of the century, with galleries and exhibit areas finding their way into smaller communities and rural communities that previously showed little or no interest in art. Several important new art museums will also be opened in the 1990s, including a spectacular new Museum of Modern Art in San Francisco and the multicultural Getty Center in Brentwood.

CALIFORNIA'S GROWING MULTICULTURALISM

With the growth of minority populations in California, the arts in the state are taking on an increasingly multicultural cast. In fact, the way in which minority and national groups have enriched California culture is already clearly evident in the institutions established in the state to preserve those contributions.

The California Center for Afro-American History and Life. Located in Oakland, this organization documents, preserves, and interprets the Afro-American experience and culture in California and the West. It is a rich repository of black history and culture in the state, with photographs and documents dating from the mid-1850s to the present time.

The Pacific Asia Museum. This institution is dedicated to furthering understanding of the people of Asia and the Pacific Rim through the arts. Its permanent collection includes some 12,000 objects, including Chinese textiles, Japanese and Chinese screens, scrolls and decorative objects. Seven different Asian ethnic arts councils celebrate their culture here with festivals and exhibits.

The Southwest Museum. This remarkable showplace, located in Los Angeles County, contains some of the finest examples of Indian art and artifacts in the United States. Permanent exhibits represent the art and culture of the native peoples of California, as well as extensive collections of Spanish colonial and Hispanic folk art.

Perhaps the most dramatic ethnic influence in California's cultural future will come from south of California's border. As the Hispanic segment of California's population reaches almost 30 percent by the end of this century, the impact of the Spanish language, and of Hispanic art and music, will be immense.

Motion pictures created to appeal to Hispanics will grow dramatically in popularity. Mexican and Central American sounds and rhythms will find their way increasingly into the music of California. Hispanic art styles and forms will have an ever greater influence on California artistic images. Spanish words and phrases will be in common usage in the California argot. Hispanic literature and periodicals will be generally available throughout the state.

THE CHANGING NATURE OF CALIFORNIA'S LIBRARIES

California is blessed with an abundance of great libraries and a state library network that is absolutely first class. The numbers are impressive: 168 public libraries with 604 branches, 192 academic libraries, and 447 special libraries. California also has extensive bookmobile services with 1,872 mobile library stops. A total of $452 million is spent annually to operate California libraries, and more than one out of every three Californians uses a library every year.[10]

What's ahead for California libraries? Lots. A $75 million bond issue voted by Californians several years ago has become the principal funding agent for library rehabilitation and expansion. Over the next several years, these funds will be allocated to renew and expand existing libraries and to build new ones. In addition to these funds, a number of cities will be financing impressive new libraries on their own. San Francisco, for instance, will build a new $98 million main library in the downtown Civic Center that will be a model for American cities. With 337,000 square feet of space, it will be twice the size of the old library it will replace. Its book capacity will be about 3 million volumes, also more than twice the capacity of the former structure.[11]

This impressive new library will typify the basic directions of California's libraries of the future.

Automation: New and present libraries will make increased use of modern communications techniques and computers. The old card-catalog system for finding books is giving way to computer cataloguing. Information discovery and retrieval will be done more on computer screens and less with books.

Diversity: Libraries in California will be expanding their role in people's cultural lives. Once a place where only books were available, the state's libraries will in the future offer a wide variety of information services, and audio and video cassettes.

Ethnicity: To serve California's growing minority populations, libraries in the state will be putting increased emphasis on language diversity in their materials. There will be special emphasis on Spanish-language books, periodicals, and audio-visual material to serve the rapidly growing Hispanic population. Multiple-language information and instructional materials will be available in almost all of California's libraries by the turn of the century.

WHEN ART BECOMES GOOD BUSINESS

It is becoming more and more obvious to communities throughout California that a vital artistic life is important when corporations and institutions decide where to locate. It is also important to people when they decide where to live and work. More than 90 percent of people say that the arts are important to the quality of life in their communities.[12]

The arts and cultural events generally are also important to the tourist industry. The availability of good theater, museums, and music is one of the principal reasons why vacationers and conventioners select California cities as their destination.

But the arts are also good business in another sense—they provide employment and civic revenue. San Francisco estimates that between 33,000 and 37,000 people are employed in full-time and part-time positions in San Francisco's arts industry. In the nonprofit segment of the arts, the total direct economic impact of arts workers is between $208 million and $240 million annually. If the economic impact of the for-profit and not-for-profit arts industries is combined, the total is about $1.3 billion.[13] That number, however, as impressive as it is, is relatively minor when compared with the impact of the arts on Los Angeles. A Los Angeles Chamber of Commerce study showed that the economy of that city is $5 billion richer because of the arts.[14]

By the year 2000, more and more of California's cities will appoint cultural task forces or similar bodies. These groups will study ways in which their cities can benefit economically by investing in artistic endeavors and cultural activities. There will be a growing civic awareness that the arts are good business.

CALIFORNIA ARTS AS A SPECTATOR SPORT

At the present time, the number of people attending cultural events—theater, opera, ballet, music, recitals, and art exhibits—is beginning to outpace the number of people who attend sports events. Between 1983 and 1987, for instance, arts spending by consumers increased more than 20 percent, while sports expenditures increased only 2 percent. Several decades ago, Californians spent twice as much on sports as on the arts. There are several reasons for this reversal.

First, the coming of age of the baby boomers has given California a whole generation of better-educated, more culturally savvy citizens. The children of that generation, now coming into young adulthood, are even more culturally oriented than their parents. Second, the growing amount of leisure time enjoyed by Californians has worked in favor of the arts. And third, the advent of culturally oriented television channels has introduced more Californians to opera, dance, theater, and classical music than ever before.

More people in California now attend the theater than attend all of California's professional sports teams. Sports still dominate the media, but more and more it is art and culture that are on the minds of Californians. This trend will undoubtedly continue through the 1990s and into the next century.

Art and sports can be expected to engage in an increasingly competitive battle for the time and dollars of Californians searching for entertainment.

However, by the year 2000, the arts in California will have clearly replaced sports as the number-one attendance industry in California.

CULTURE AND ART AT HOME

Some of the most outstanding private collections of fine art in American history have been in California homes. Legendary California collectors of the past have included Dore Schary, Edward G. Robinson, and Armand Hammer. The trend of outstanding private art continues today in California: Margaret and Harry Anderson (modern and contemporary art), Donald Bren (twentieth-century art), Phoebe Cowles (European still life), Doris and Peter Drucker (Japanese paintings), David Geffen (modern art), David Bermant (technological art), Walter Annenberg (Impressionist painting), and Jack Nicholson (U.S. and European art). They are among the many Californians who constitute one of the world's largest groups of private collectors.

One Santa Monica man has followed the trend toward in-home culture to the extreme. Aaron Mendelsohn, a classical music fan, has turned the major part of his house into a 100-seat concert hall. He built his new home around a 1,200-square-foot hall with a spotlit stage, soundproof walls, and a 25-foot-high ceiling, carefully engineered for classical chamber music. His opening concert in early 1991, staged for invited friends and guests, featured the music of Chopin and Mozart.[16]

Gordon Getty, known both for his wealth and for his interest in the arts, has obtained permission from the City of San Francisco to build an amphitheater attached to his home in Pacific Heights. With seating for up to several hundred, the new Getty Hall is expected to present theatrical and musical entertainments for the Gettys' friends and associates. Some of the music featured in these presentations will no doubt be the creation of Mr. Getty himself, a noted composer in his own right.

The trend toward the enjoyment of art and of cultural activities in the home will continue throughout the 1990s—not just among the wealthy, but among Californians of all circumstances. Sales of fine art reproductions, videocassettes of the performing arts, recorded music and lectures, art magazines and periodicals will all enjoy a boom in this decade as part of the trend toward enjoying culture on one's own terms.

MOVIES AND TELEVISION: WHERE CALIFORNIA IS THE CAPITAL OF THE WORLD

Seventy years ago, California's fledgling movie industry in Hollywood produced 90 percent of the world's movies. Soon motion picture production became the fifth-largest industry in America. Hollywood's near-monopoly ended some years ago, but the state still remains the dominant force in film making. In 1988, California was responsible for 211 of 383 feature films produced in the United States. In terms of revenues, California feature films produced about $4 billion in income, almost 65 percent of all U.S. motion picture revenue.[17] In fact, the film industry, which at one point seemed to be gravitating away from the state, has returned to California in dramatic fashion. The number of feature films made in California has more than doubled since the mid-1980s.

Of even greater importance is the manner in which California-produced film and film images now dominate the world market. Income from film rental to foreign countries by the major American film studios exceeds $1.5 billion.[18] Japan is the largest importer of American films, followed by Canada, France, and West Germany.

California's dominance of the American and world television market is even more pronounced. American-produced television programs dominate the screens of countries throughout the civilized world. The overwhelming majority of these programs are produced in the studios of Southern California.

As if to reinforce its importance as an art force in California, the motion picture industry has recently opened the Academy of Motion Picture Arts and Sciences Center for Motion Picture Study. Located in Beverly Hills, the center houses a major, comprehensive collection of motion pictures, as well as 5 million photographs, 18,000 books and periodicals, and 5,000 scripts. In all, over 12,000 films are available for study and viewing. The Center has a full-time staff of 32 librarians and archivists.[19]

California's dominance in the film and television industry will continue well into the next century. The skills required to produce quality shows are found in California to a far greater degree than anywhere else, and the state will continue to be a magnet for the best talent from around the world.

CALIFORNIA'S CULTURAL CENTERS

One trend is clear in California's cultural future. The state will have more local and regional centers that offer multiple cultural activities.

The prototype center was built in Costa Mesa in 1986. The Orange County Performing Arts Center, constructed at a cost of almost $75 million, includes museums, theaters, art galleries, and educational facilities. Other such centers quickly followed.

In February of 1991, the city of Mountain View on the San Francisco Peninsula opened its beautiful new Center for the Performing Arts. The center houses a 623-seat proscenium theater with a full balcony, as well as a performance room that will hold 200 people. The center is now finishing an amphitheater with lawn seating for 300. Part of a new municipal complex that includes the city hall, the Center for the Performing Arts will offer as many as 350 performances a year.[20] It is eloquent testimony to the culture-consciousness of this small city of just 60,000 residents in Silicon Valley.

Walnut Creek in the San Francisco Bay Area has just opened its own Regional Center for Arts, the result of ten years of planning and fund-raising. Its main theater will feature a variety of artistic and cultural events, while its 3,550 square-foot exhibition hall will feature exhibits of sculpture, drawings, paintings, and prints.[21]

Still other centers are in the planning stage. Sometime in the next few years, San Francisco expects to build the Yerba Buena Gardens Cultural Center as the centerpiece of a new development on twenty-one acres of three downtown sites on Market Street.[22]

The High Desert Cultural Art Center will soon be built in Apple Valley. The present architectural plans call for a 1,500- to 2,000-seat theater, an art gallery, workshops for cultural art groups, and even a spacious arboretum/ conservatory for the floral arts.[23]

The concept of the area cultural center, a headquarters complex for different disciplines in the arts, will become even more popular in California by the year 2000 than it is today. As many as a dozen different districts in the state will either be building or planning such a center by the start of the new century.

THE CALIFORNIA ARTS COUNCIL

Established in 1976 by the California Legislature, the California Arts Council started life with a small staff and a modest appropriation with the stated purpose of "giving the arts their rightful place in the lives of the California people."[24] In the intervening years, its budget has increased from less than $1.5 million to more than $14 million. The Council has established an artists-in-residence program, supported city and county arts councils, and made grants to more than 1,000 organizations as well as individual artists.[25]

At its outset, the Arts Council was extremely controversial because of its unorthodox leadership and its disdain for traditional art forms. But through the past decade it has settled in as a useful force in developing artistic talents in California and in making the state art-conscious at the local level. It has also concentrated some of its efforts toward developing art programs in schools.

The goal of the Council is to become a more significant driving force in the California art world and to improve its funding. It looks forward to a budget of $1.00 for every California resident by the year

2000, which would bring its funding to $35 million. It is very doubtful if it can achieve this aim without a dramatic, unforeseen reversal of current budgetary restraints at the state level. However, the Arts Council has a worthy role to play and could well become a major vehicle for ensuring that the arts in California continue to flourish.

WHO WILL PAY FOR CALIFORNIA'S ARTS?

The arts in many other parts of the world are largely government supported, but the arts in California must look for their patronage elsewhere. A recent study by the San Francisco Foundation showed that arts organizations earned 56 percent of their total income from presentation revenue, that is, admissions and ticket sales, memberships, and dues. The other 44 percent came in the form of contributions from individuals, foundations, corporations, and, to a far lesser extent, government.[26]

In the past decade, corporate participation in the major cultural disciplines, especially opera, ballet, symphony, and museums, was impressive. California corporations during the 1980s contributed an estimated $800 million to artistic activities in the state, with Chevron, Pacific Telesis, Times-Mirror, and Nissan Motors leading the way. The most giving California foundations were the Mengart Foundation, the Wallace Alexander Gerbode Foundations, the James Irvine Foundation, and the San Francisco Foundation. Among the private California citizens who were especially generous to the arts during the decade were Armand Hammer, Gordon Getty, Walter Annenberg, and the Otis Chandler family.

It is likely that there will be a serious shift during the 1990s in the way the arts in California are funded. In all likelihood, arts organizations will have to be less reliant on contributory sources and far more dependent on their immediate audiences.

Coming out of a recessionary period and into a period in which profit recovery will be all-important, business will feel far less generous in areas that do not directly relate to income. Government, no more than a minor player now in the arts, will be even less so in the future. With tax revenues down at the city, county, and state levels, and with intense pressures not to reduce social programs, allocation for arts and for cultural activities will be in an ever-tightening vise. Higher taxes at both the state and local level will tend to stifle individual contributions.

Between now and the year 2000, the California arts will be far more dependent on their own audiences for their well-being. Ticket and admission sales may constitute 75 to 80 percent of all arts income by the end of the decade. This means that those performing arts capable of achieving the greatest popular appeal will be the ones that will prosper. Cultural forms and activities that have limited or historical appeal will have a much more difficult time thriving—even surviving—in the decade ahead.

BY THE YEAR 2000:

It is almost certain that:

- California will be, more than ever, the center of activity for painters, artists, and sculptors, with the Los Angeles area as the epicenter.
- More than 400,000 Californians will call themselves "working artists" in various fields.
- The $360 million Getty Center, which will include a museum, a center for the study of art history, a state-of-the-art conservation institute, and underground parking for 1,200 art lovers, will open on a 110-acre site in Brentwood.
- San Franciscans will spend $60 million to create a spectacular five-story Museum of Modern Art containing 200,000 square feet of museum space.
- Los Angeles will spend $35 million to renovate the Hollywood Bowl.
- Walt Disney Concert Hall, the new futuristic 2,350-seat home of the Los Angeles Philharmonic, which will house a museum of Disney and Philharmonic memorabilia, will be finished at a cost of over $110 million and open for business.

- San Francisco will build and open a new $98 million library in its Civic Center containing twice the space of the former library, quintupling the seating capacity, and housing more than 3 million volumes.
- Hispanic culture will be much more prominent in California art, films, literature, and music.

It is very likely that:

- Opera will be more popular than ever in California, and San Diego will establish an important new opera company.
- Concord will build a new $14 million, 20,000-seat amphitheater for the performing arts, as well as a 75,000-square-foot exhibition hall.
- Motion picture companies in California will produce more than 300 first-run films each year at a cost of $2.5 billion.
- Davies Hall, home of the San Francisco Symphony, will have spent more than $30 million improving its acoustics.
- Disney will open a new $3 billion entertainment and educational center in Anaheim that will attract more than 20 million visitors a year.
- Sacramento, San Francisco, Los Angeles, and San Diego will all have built major new central libraries in their downtown areas.
- A new $30 million Museum of Mexican Art, with 70,000 square feet of exhibition space, will be built in San Francisco.
- New ballet companies in California will be headquartered in Sacramento and San Diego.

It is even possible that:

- There will be some 50 new symphony orchestras in California.
- Several hundred new art galleries will be opened throughout the state.
- The Golden Gate Bridge will build, at a cost of $3 million, a privately financed historical museum depicting the building of the bridge.

- California will pioneer and produce computer books, small cassettes that slip into hand-held computers that show the text of the book on an easily read screen.
- Some California cities will require developers of commercial real estate to spend as much as 2 percent of their project costs on "public art" such as sculpture, murals, and paintings.
- The state appropriation for the California Arts Council will exceed $20 million.
- The number of motion picture screens in California will increase from 2,950 to almost 4,000.
- California cities will once again make major investments in the arts in the belief that it is good business.

12

California and Political Power

This will be a watershed decade for politics in California. Historic changes will take place both in state government and in California's impact on national government. The forces bringing about this change are the explosive growth of California's population as measured by the national census of 1990, the desire for change as expressed in recent public referenda, and the shifting political character of the state as reflected in recent elections and polls.

CALIFORNIA WILL BE AN AWESOME PRESENCE IN THE NATION'S CAPITAL

The recent national census showed that the United States population had grown to some 250 million, an increase of more than 10 percent over the previous census a decade earlier. It also showed that California, already the country's largest state, enjoyed a 26 percent increase over that same period and had a population of some 30 million.[1] These census figures are, of course, used to reapportion the 435 seats in the House of Representatives among the 50 states to reflect relative gains or losses during the previous ten years.

The 1990 census will give California seven additional seats in the House, raising the state's total from 45 to 52, more seats than any state has ever had before. Put another way, California will have more representatives than twenty-one other states combined. It also means that California will cast 12 percent of the total votes in the House of Representatives throughout the 1990s.

The state's elected congressmen, of course, are not a single entity and can rarely, if ever, be expected to vote together as a bloc. But they will represent a formidable force in the Congress, even though they will be split politically.

When it comes to issues involving the well-being of California in which most California representatives can be expected to act with a mutuality of interest, the new delegation will have tremendous clout. And in any vote, the Californians will be tough to ignore, tougher still to sidestep.

If the California delegation is a powerhouse in the 1990s, imagine what will be after the census of the year 2000! If California gains a minimum of the additional 5 to 6 million residents forecast for the decade, then California could pick up still another seven to eight seats as we enter the next century.

For the first decade of the twenty-first century, California could have as many as sixty seats in the House of Representatives, accounting for almost one out of every seven votes in the House of Representatives.

After the year 2000, California will have more votes in the House than twenty-three other states combined, a measure of political clout probably not contemplated by the authors of the Constitution.

CALIFORNIA AND THE SUN BELT WILL SET THE POLITICAL AGENDA FOR THE NEXT CENTURY

America's population, and with it the nation's political power, is clearly shifting to the West and the South. A look at the change in the population of the nation makes this clearly evident.

This trend will continue throughout the 1990s. By the year 2000, the political power shift will be even more pronounced than it is now. The Sun Belt, dominated by California itself, will set the social and political agenda for the rest of this century and into the next.

FIGURE 12-1
U.S. POPULATION GROWTH BY REGION, 1980–1990

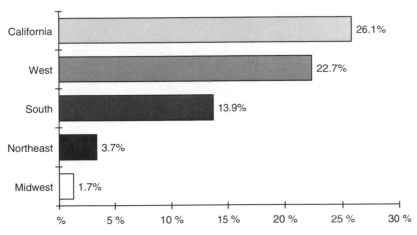

Source: U.S. Bureau of the Census.

Political reapportionment for the 1990s will give the West and South fifteen additional congressional seats, most of them subtracted from the Northeast. Added to the seats they already have, this means that 56 percent of the House of Representatives will be from the Sun Belt. Four states—California, Arizona, Texas, and Florida—will control more than 25 percent of all congressional seats.[2]

Issues important to older, more established states, including the revival of smokestack industries and the renewal of inner cities, will be put on the back burner. Pushed to the forefront will be concerns of the newer, faster-growing, warm-weather states. These include:

Water: the development and distribution of water resources for states growing in population and producing agricultural products for the rest of the country.

Environment: the preservation of natural resources, wilderness areas, national and regional parks, old-growth forests.

Immigration: control over the borders of the country, barring illegal immigrants, permitting the entrance of people with needed skills.

Roads: building the highways, roadways, and infrastructure to service new and expanding communities in the growing states.

Power: developing the electrical and other power needs necessary to service the expanding populations of the country.

One major test of the new power of the Sun Belt states will be the struggle to determine whether federal funds go primarily to the repair of old roads and highways or to the construction of new highways. Look for California and the other growth states to win this fight and other political battles throughout the decade and into the next century.

THE IMPORTANCE OF THE YEAR 1992

Reapportionment, term limits, retirements, political succession— all these set the stage for the most crowded and explosive year that California politics has ever seen. As one observer remarked, "California has become a political Disneyland, and everyone wants an E ticket!"[3] Here are some of the excitements that await California voters in 1992:

A presidential race, with California holding 10 percent of the votes in both the primary and the election.

Two simultaneous U.S. Senate races, for the first time in memory, with literally dozens of candidates declaring for the two available seats.

Seven new seats in the House, with redistricting that will throw at least another eight more seats up for grabs. In a typical congressional cycle, there may be only two dozen House seats nationally that are really seriously contended. There may be that many this time in California alone.

Nervous state legislators, suddenly aware, because of Proposition 140, that they cannot be lifetime legislators, will be trying to move up the ladder or making plans to move out. As many as 27 of the 80 Assembly seats may have no incumbent running.

The cost of the U.S. Senate campaigns in California alone is expected to reach $75 million.[4] Including the presidential primaries and elections, campaign spending in the state for the year could reach the astronomical sum of half a billion dollars! As George

Gorton, Governor Wilson's campaign manager, has said, "There's nothing comparable at any time in any state in America."[5]

What happens in 1992 will have a tremendous effect on California in the year 2000. The odds are that the two elected U.S. senators will still be in office at the turn of the century. An overwhelming majority of the 52 members elected to the Congress from the redistricted California map will still be representing their constituencies in the nation's capital at the end of the century. (Congressmen have a 98 percent reelection rate, and the next redistricting will not take place until the year 2001.) And any national candidate who demonstrates an ability to pull votes in California will find himself in a strong position to make a presidential run for the term that will encompass the year 2000.

CALIFORNIA WILL NOMINATE PRESIDENTS

For several decades, the California presidential primaries in early June have played an important but not usually pivotal role in the selection of presidential candidates. By the time the party faithful troop to the polls in California, the field is generally down to a few candidates. Not infrequently, the choice has already been made by voters in other, smaller states, and California voters have only the dubious glory of confirming their party's predetermined choice.

All this will change by the year 2000. Sometime in the 1990s, the state legislature will vote to advance the California primary to the month of March. This means that the California primary, coming early in the presidential campaigns and determining almost one out of every eight votes at the party conventions, will be the key factor in determining who the eventual party candidates will be.

Problems still remain in the effort to advance the California primary. Republicans in the legislature are anxious to remove state initiatives and referenda from any primary vote, fearing that a primary would bring out more Democrats than Republicans. Also, the cost of an additional vote could be as high as $40 million,[6] not a small consideration in a tight budget era. These obstacles will be overcome, however, and California's political importance will be reinforced by an early state primary that will be instrumental in determining who the national candidates will be.

CALIFORNIA WILL ELECT PRESIDENTS

For many decades now, it has been difficult to win the presidency without winning California. Since 1912, only one candidate, Jimmy Carter, has won the presidency without carrying California.

The importance of California in future presidential campaigns will be absolutely critical. In 1992, for instance, California will cast more than 10 percent of all the votes in the Electoral College. In the election of 2004, California will probably cast 13 to 15 percent of all the votes when the College meets to name the new president.

This means that, in the future even more than in the past, the presidential campaign time and money that national candidates spend in California will be extraordinary. It is possible that as much as $100 million will be spent in California by the presidential candidates alone in 1992. By the year 2000, that amount could reach $200 million.

This will be money well spent, for whoever carries the state of California will stand an overwhelming chance of becoming the president of the United States.

CALIFORNIA CASH WILL FUEL ELECTIONS ELSEWHERE

In recent decades, California has meant more than just votes to America's political parties. It has also meant money. As great as the financial needs of California political candidates themselves are, there seems to be plenty of California cash left over to fuel elections elsewhere. With the exception of New York State, California exported more funds in the last election than any other state. In all,

Californians contributed almost $8 million to the campaign efforts of candidates in other parts of the country.[7]

Remarkably, more than 500 congressional candidates—most of them incumbents—financed their campaigns last year from outside their own states. For many of them, Californians provided the funds that meant the margin of victory. As California continues to grow in population and in wealth in relation to other states, even more candidates outside the state will look to California for the funds they need to campaign successfully. In 1992, there will be great cash needs in California itself because of the coincidence of so many expensive campaigns taking place at the same time. But after that, California money will continue to push beyond the state borders in ever larger amounts.

By the year 2000, Californians will be contributing more than $15 million in election years to influence political campaigns in other states, and California will be regarded as the number one source for out-of-state funds by politicians all across America.

THE STATE LEGISLATURE: OUT WITH THE OLD, IN WITH THE NEW!

In the fall of 1990, California voters passed Proposition 140 by a comfortable majority. This proposition restricts Assembly members to six years in office, state senators and statewide elected officials to eight years.[8] Court challenges to Proposition 140 on the grounds that it deprives voters of their free and open choice on the ballot will fail. Barring unforeseen developments, this proposition spells the end of the professional, lifetime legislator who makes his or her presence in the California Assembly or Senate a full-time career.

If Proposition 140 is fully implemented, as now seems likely, not a single member now serving in the California Assembly will be in office past the year 1996, and not a single state senator currently serving will be in office by the year 1998.

In most cases, "lifetime politicians" will be replaced by "citizen legislators" who come from varied backgrounds. It is expected that the new legislature will probably be somewhat older, as many retired or experienced businessmen, educators, and private citizens stand for election. It may also be chaotic, as officeholders less experienced in negotiation and compromise push their own agendas and argue their private platforms. The role of lobbyists may also be enhanced as these less experienced legislators seek information and counsel on pending laws and regulations.

But no matter what the character of any future legislative body in Sacramento, the year 2000 will see completely new faces in both the Assembly and Senate. In fact, at the start of the new century, these new members of the Assembly will themselves already be more than halfway through their time in office.

POWER TO THE PEOPLE

One of the major political struggles in California during the 1990s will be between growing ethnic minorities attempting to gain representation and entrenched office-holders trying to retain power for themselves. It is now clear that California's minority groups, especially the mushrooming Hispanic and Asian populations, will gain substantial empowerment by the year 2000.

Early in 1991, the U.S. Supreme Court let stand a historic Los Angeles County redistricting plan that paved the way for its first Latino supervisor in this century. The finding was that the all-Anglo Board of Supervisors discriminated against Hispanics in drawing district boundaries a decade earlier.[9] The decision left in place a new political map that favors representation for the county's minority residents. This decision, as well as earlier court decisions in other parts of California, makes it clear that future districting of the state's counties and cities will have to be done with minority representation in mind.

With the Hispanic population approaching 30 percent by the start of the next century and the Asian population accounting for almost 12 percent, it is obvious that office-holders representing these groups will be more and more prominent in the halls of

power throughout the state, especially at the county level, but also on city boards and in the state legislature. California's minority populations will take their rightful place in government at all levels.

CALIFORNIA'S GROWING CONSERVATISM

The two major political parties are perhaps as contentious in California as anywhere in the United States. Sixty years ago, registered voters were heavily Republican, representing almost three-quarters of the electorate. Within just ten years, Democrats, primarily as a result of the Depression, effected an almost complete turnabout, gaining almost 60 percent of all those registered. The Democratic party has maintained its dominance ever since.

Nevertheless, Republicans, despite their minority position among registered voters, have had remarkable success in electing their candidates to top leadership positions.

Republicans have held the governorship of the state for over a decade. With one exception California has voted for the Republican presidential candidate for the past twenty-five years. It should also be noted that the Republican party has gained among registered voters every year since 1980.

TABLE 12-1

CALIFORNIA VOTER REGISTRATION, 1930–1990

Year	Democrat	Republican	Other
1930	20.3	73.0	6.7
1940	59.7	36.0	4.3
1950	58.4	37.1	4.6
1960	57.5	39.2	3.3
1970	54.9	39.8	5.2
1980	53.2	34.7	12.1
1984	52.0	36.5	10.4
1986	50.8	38.3	10.9
1988	50.4	38.6	11.0
1990	49.9	39.0	11.0

Source: Office of the Secretary of State.

The present trend toward Republicanism in California is further evidenced by the fact that more California voters now identify with the Republican party than with the Democratic. In response to the question, "Do you think of yourself as a Republican, a Democrat, an independent or what?" 5 percent more Californians proclaimed themselves to be Republicans than said they were Democrats. When the "leaners" are added, Republicans still led 48 to 45 percent.

TABLE 12-2

CALIFORNIA VOTERS' SELF-IDENTIFICATION BY PARTY

Republican	39%
Independent—leans Republican	9%
Independent/other	9%
Independent—leans Democrat	11%
Democrat	34%

Source: The California Poll and California Almanac, Fifth Edition.

It is very likely that, barring a national economic calamity, this trend toward Republicanism will continue through the 1990s. Republican candidates, especially those running for congressional seats, will fare well in California through the year 2000.

There are several reasons for this trend. First, the population growth in California on which the new apportionment will be based has been primarily in the southern and inland portions of the state, both of which tend to be more conservative and hence more Republican. Five of the seven new seats will, in fact, go to Southern California, where growth has been largely in the suburban areas. Two new seats in Northern California will most probably be needed to accommodate the soaring populations in the San Joaquin Valley around Sacramento and in the new suburban communities east of San Francisco Bay.[10]

The second factor indicating a Republican resurgence in the congressional delegation is the fact that a Republican governor has been able to influence the redistricting. In 1980, the congressional districts were drawn by a Democratic legislature and approved by a Democratic governor, much to the detriment of the Republicans. This time, the redistricting was done by a panel of supposedly impartial judges and has thus far been affirmed by the courts. There is a consensus that the new plan should produce dramatic gains for the Republican party in the next election.

But regardless of the eventual makeup of the California congressional delegation at the turn of the century, it will almost certainly be more conservative in nature and more responsive to the needs and desires of Southern and inland Californians.

A NEW POLITICAL "FAULT LINE" FOR CALIFORNIA

Californians, over the past several decades, have become accustomed to thinking of elections in the state as contests between Northern California and Southern California. Historically, the northern cities and counties tend to be liberal and Democratic, while those in the southern part of the state tend to be more conservative and hence more Republican. However, the north versus south concept of election politics is now undergoing dramatic change.

Recent elections, as well as the population shift within the state, indicate that the political "fault line" in the future will no longer divide north from south, but rather east from west.

The clearest recent example of this change was in the last gubernatorial election. Republican Pete Wilson won all but three of the state's forty inland counties. Democrat Dianne Feinstein won the overwhelming majority of all the counties on or near the coast, including Los Angeles County. In fact, if favorite-son Wilson had not carried his home county of San Diego, the east versus west nature of the contest would have been even more pronounced. A look at the county-by-county breakdown of the race shows clearly the changing nature of the California electorate.

The east-west fault line will be even more pronounced in statewide elections of the future. The booming inland counties of California, especially those in the Central Valley, the Sierra foothills, and the southeast corner of the state, will bring a tide of conservative votes to statewide elections. Voters in the coastal

counties will tend to be more liberal in comparison with those in
the rest of the state. Effective political planning in the year 2000
will require a clear understanding of this fundamental change in
the California political landscape.

FIGURE 12-2
VOTE FOR GOVERNOR BY COUNTY, 1990

Source: New York Times News Service.

"ANYWHERE BUT CALIFORNIA"

Resentment of California's growing political muscle is already surfacing in other states, as well as in the nation's capital. The ABC syndrome (Anywhere But California) is already in full flower in the nation's capital. Legislators from other states fight often and vigorously to diminish the impact of California's voting power on national legislation. Money earmarked for California highways, mass transit, or environment is usually contested strongly by established interests from other states. Defense contracts come less frequently to California. The recent granting of the contract for the advanced tactical fighter to Lockheed instead of Northrop, for example, will cost the state thousands of jobs. Washington gave the $8 billion supercollider project to Texas instead of California. Almost a dozen major California installations were high on the recent list of closings of military establishments.

The ABC Syndrome will only intensify in the years ahead as the power and influence of California make themselves felt in the corridors of national power. By the end of the century, resentment of California and of its political strength will be epidemic in Washington, D.C., as well as in the legislative bodies of neighboring states. California's representatives will have to fight energetically to see that the state is not shortchanged legislatively in the Congress and by the Washington bureaucracy. But in the long run, the political might of California in the twenty-first century will be irresistible.

BY THE YEAR 2000:

It is almost certain that:

- The census will give California almost 60 seats in the House of Representatives, representing almost one of every seven votes in the Congress.
- The number of Hispanic politicians and officeholders will have increased dramatically throughout the state, especially in the southern counties.

- Not a single present-day member of the California State Assembly or State Senate will still be in office.
- The California presidential primary will be held in March instead of July.
- The new census will indicate that California should have 13.5 percent of the Electoral College.
- Asians will be elected to public office in increasing numbers both at the state and local levels.

It is very likely that:

- The presidential candidates chosen in the California primary will be nominated at both conventions.
- More than $500 million will be spent on political campaigns in California during national election years.
- The number of California counties with more registered Republicans than Democrats will increase from 14 to 20.
- At least 90 percent of the California delegation to the House of Representatives elected in 1992 will still be in office.
- Californians will send up to $20 million in cash to out-of-state office seekers.
- The two U.S. senators elected in 1992 will still be in office.

It is even possible that:

- Someone you have not yet heard of will be the governor of California.
- The percentage of registered voters who vote in the presidential election will fall below 50 percent.
- Severe restrictions will be placed on political contributions by lobbying organizations.
- More than 25 percent of all Californians will vote by absentee ballot.
- The Republican party will be the dominant party in the state.
- For the second time in history, a Californian will be president of the United States.

13

California in the Twenty-First Century

It is difficult to contemplate what California may be like in the next century without a sense of wonder and astonishment. The trends in population growth, in economic development, and in political potential all lead to the inescapable conclusion that California will be a powerhouse almost beyond imagining.

Of course, a number of factors are difficult if not impossible to predict, and any one or combination of these unknowables could dramatically affect any forecast for California. Will the seemingly unstoppable influx of people to California crowd its cities and highways to a point where California becomes a less desirable and attractive place to live? Will a shortage of water put a halt to California's agricultural and manufacturing productivity? Will California's rapidly changing ethnic makeup put too great a stress on its social fabric? Does California have some sort of cataclysm in its future—an earthquake of a magnitude that could seriously alter the state's fortunes? Anyone brave enough to forecast California's future beyond the year 2000 runs the risk of having one or more of these imponderables throw his or her predictions off line.

Yet, there are some things about California in the next century that seem virtually certain. The state will have many more people and will become a great deal more crowded. It will become more diverse in population and culture. There will be greater strains on its systems and on its infrastructure. It will become more powerful politically. Both its problems and its opportunities will grow, along with its population.

Here, then, are some fearless forecasts of where California might be at certain points through the first half of the twenty-first century.

Some are based on reliable statistical information, some on projecting present trends into the future, some on informed guess, some on inspired hunch. Be that as it may, it is entirely possible that:

BY THE YEAR 2010:

- Forty million people will live in California.
- The Southwest states will have more than 60 percent of America's total population.
- California's population will be 46 percent white, 33 percent Hispanic, 14 percent Asian, and 7 percent black.
- Sacramento will be the sixth-largest city in America.
- The population of Los Angeles County will exceed the population of New York State.
- Area codes in California will have four numbers.
- The "baby boom" generation will be approaching retirement age.
- The state will have 2.5 million high school students.
- Women will constitute almost half of California's total work force.
- More than 20 percent of all the new homes built in the United States will be built in California.
- The average Californian will be four years younger than the average American.
- All employers with five or more people will be required to offer health insurance to their workers.
- Half the telephones in California will be unlisted.
- There will be more than 20 million jobs in California.
- There will be more than 15 million households in the state.
- New desert national parks will be established in California, including a 4.5-million-acre Mojave Desert Park and a 3.3-million-acre Death Valley Park.
- The cost of the average single-family house in California will be over $500,000.
- The average California male will live to be 78, and the average California female will live to be 82.
- New office buildings will be required to install two complete sets of plumbing, one for reclaimed water, another for drinking water.
- Californians will replace residents of Massachusetts as the most heavily taxed people in America.

- Twenty percent of all California automobiles will be electrically powered.
- A postage stamp will cost one dollar.
- California will spend up to $3 million a year in attempting to catch "water rustlers" who illegally siphon off and divert water from state creeks and reservoirs.
- The California State Lottery will be discontinued.
- Fifteen million people annually will fly the air corridor between Los Angeles and the Bay Area.
- The school year will last 210 days.
- California will be building a new public school somewhere in the state every week.
- Portable classrooms, used to house overflow students in overcrowded state school districts, will be in common use in California.
- SAT scores of California public school students will drop to a new all-time low. California business will take on the job of "reeducating" young people so that they can enter the work force.
- The state's Asian population will exceed 6 million.
- Californians will own more than 30 million automobiles.
- The new census will give California 65 seats in the House of Representatives.
- The San Joaquin Valley will replace the Los Angeles Basin as the smog capital of America.
- The University of California will have four additional campuses.
- More than 200,000 Californians will be in prison.
- It will cost ten dollars to cross the Golden Gate bridge.
- Use of the AIDS vaccine will be so widespread that the disease will no longer pose a serious threat to Californians.
- Californians will be bracing themselves for another major earthquake.

BY THE YEAR 2020:

- Almost 50 million people will be living in California.
- Virtually all of the increased population of California over the previous decade will be Hispanic or Asian.

- The population of the state will be 40 percent white, 38 percent Hispanic, 16 percent Asian, and 6 percent black.
- The "baby boom" generation will be enjoying active retirement.
- A completely self-contained artificial heart will be routinely implanted in Californians to replace diseased human hearts.
- So many Californians will reach the age of 100 that they will no longer get their names in the paper when they do.
- There will be almost 23 million jobs in California, almost 15 percent of all the jobs in America.
- The economy of California will be larger than that of all but three nations in the world.
- Nine different California counties will have more than one million residents.
- A quarter of a million Californians will be in prison.
- Hot tubs will be illegal.
- California farmers will be growing a number of fruits and vegetables that do not exist now, including apples that taste like pears; seedless, bite-sized plums; cheese-flavored cauliflower.
- Only half of the vehicles on California highways will use gasoline.
- The average speed on most metropolitan expressways will not exceed three miles per hour during peak drive-times.
- The number of students in California schools will be almost double the number at the turn of the century.
- There will be about 10,000 new schools in California.
- The average California home will cost over $700,000.
- Only one-third of California households will be married-couple families.
- Road signs in Southern California will be in both English and Spanish.
- An AIDS cure will be available for Californians who neglected to have themselves inoculated.
- The new census will give California 68 seats in the House of Representatives, representing almost 1 out of every 6 votes in the House.
- California will have its first Republican, Hispanic governor in over a century and a half.
- Birthrates in California will be dropping as a result of widespread use of the male contraceptive pill and the "morning after" abortion pill.

- A hotel room at one of California's luxury resorts will cost more than one thousand dollars a day.
- Some 10,000 Californians will be murdered during the year.
- Water rationing will be mandatory for all Californians, regardless of their location in the state.
- Seven major new airports will have been built in the state.
- Only 25 percent of California's land surface will be farmland.
- The latest public referendum to split California into two states will have once again passed in the north and failed in the south.
- Californians will be bracing themselves for another major earthquake.

BY THE YEAR 2050:

- There will be 65 to 70 million people living in California.
- Two out of every nine Americans will be a Californian.
- The Hispanic population in California will be larger than the white population.
- California will have at least three cities with populations of over 500,000 that did not exist in the year 2000.
- Three of the five largest cities in the United States will be in California.
- Los Angeles will be the largest city in the world.
- The life expectancy of the average Californian will exceed 80 years.
- Someone born in the twenty-first century will be elected governor of the state.
- The average single-family house in California will cost more than one million dollars.
- Californians will own more than 40 million automobiles.
- Seventy percent of all vehicles on California highways will be electrically powered.
- Atomic energy will once again be in the ascendancy, partly because it is needed to generate electricity for California's cars.
- The speed limit on the new high-speed highway system will be 100 miles per hour.
- There will be two additional bridges over San Francisco Bay.
- A round of golf at Pebble Beach will cost a thousand dollars, and reservations will have to be made at least six months in advance.

- Poplar trees will provide a major source of liquid fuels for automobiles and for manufacturing equipment in California.
- A plane flight from San Francisco to Los Angeles will take twenty minutes.
- Hot tubs will again be legalized.
- Gambling will be legal in California.
- One-fourth of all the members of the House of Representatives will be Californians.
- The state will have seven regional governments with jurisdiction over transportation, air quality, water supplies, and general environmental matters.
- Water rationing will be year-round and will be controlled by the state.
- A new state cultural center, housing a world-class opera house, a major ballet theater, a series of exhibit galleries, a number of theaters, and a symphony hall will be built just outside Sacramento, the fourth-largest city in the United States.
- A permit will be required to enter three or four of California's most populous cities by car.
- Los Angeles County will be larger than all but four states.
- California will annex part of the Baja Peninsula.
- California will be granted ''superstate'' status by the U.S. Congress, with special privileges including the right to restrict immigration and the right to revise federal legislation as it affects California.
- Californians will be bracing themselves for the next major earthquake.

The author reserves the right to be wrong on any of these specific forecasts, but feels confident that his batting average will be high. Why not stick around and see for yourself?

References

CHAPTER ONE

1. *The Bay of San Francisco, A History,* Lewis Publishing Company, Chicago, IL, 1892, p. 179.
2. Samuel Dickson, *Tales of San Francisco,* Stanford University Press, Stanford, CA, 1947, p. 15.
3. *Bicentennial Edition, Historical Statistics of the United States,* U.S. Department of Commerce, Washington, D.C., 1975, p. 25.
4. *Ibid.*
5. *Ibid.*
6. Dan Walters, ''The 'New' California,'' *California History,* Winter Edition, 1989/90, p. 227.
7. *Bicentennial Edition, Historical Statistics of the United States,* p. 25.
8. ''State Says Population Is 30 Million Tomorrow,'' *San Francisco Chronicle,* September 8, 1990.
9. Joseph Henry Jackson, *Western Gate,* Farrar, Straus and Young, New York, 1952, p. 107.
10. Frank Soulé, John H. Gihon, M.D., and James Nisbet, *The Annals of San Francisco,* D. Appleton and Company, New York, 1854, p. 176.
11. Oscar Lewis, *The Big Four,* Alfred A. Knopf, New York, 1946, pp. 73–74.
12. *Population Projections for California Counties, 1980–2020,* California Department of Finance, Sacramento, CA, 1986, p. 2.
13. *Estimates of Refugees in California Counties and the State,* California Department of Finance, 1990, pp. 1–3.
14. Carol Ness, ''The un-whitening of California,'' *San Francisco Examiner,* April 14, 1991.
15. John Gunther, *Inside USA,* Harper & Brothers, New York, 1947, p. 2.
16. Ken Dychtwald, *Age Wave,* Bantam Books, New York, 1990, pp. 4, 5.

17. *Ibid.*, p. 6.
18. Interview with Hans P. Johnson, Research Analyst, California Department of Finance, on October 23, 1990.
19. *Ibid.*
20. *Ibid.*
21. *Ibid.*
22. *California Population Characteristics,* Center for Continuing Study of the California Economy, Palo Alto, CA, 1991, pp. 22, 23.
23. "100-Year-Olds: A Living Treasure," *Senior Spectrum,* February 8, 1989.
24. *California Population Characteristics,* pp. 13, 14.
25. "California still most urban state in country," *San Francisco Examiner,* December 18, 1991.
26. *California Population Characteristics*, pp. viii–x.
27. Ricardo Chavira, "Hatred, Fear and Vigilance," *Time Magazine,* November 19, 1990, p. 12.
28. "S.F. Led Jump In Housing Costs," *San Francisco Chronicle,* May 10, 1991.
29. Interview with Lance C. Barnett, director of the Office of Economic Research, California Department of Commerce, October 22, 1990.

CHAPTER TWO

1. "California," *The Economist,* October 13, 1990, p. 3.
2. Interview with Lance Barnett, Office of Economic Research, California Department of Commerce, October 28, 1990.
3. *California Almanac, Fifth Edition,* Pacific Data Resources, Santa Barbara, CA, 1991, pp. 336–48.
4. *Vision: California 2010,* California Economic Development Corporation, A Special Report to the Governor, 1988, p. 10.
5. *Ibid.*, p. 19.
6. *Ibid.*, p. 20.
7. *Economic Report of the Governor, State of California, 1989.*
8. *Ibid.*
9. *Economic and Business Outlook,* Bank of America, March 1989.
10. Hilary Johnston Barton, "Defense Department and California," *California Magazine,* January 1991, p. 12.
11. *Vision: California 2010,* p. 14.
12. *California Almanac, Fifth Edition,* pp. 424, 429, 449.
13. *Ibid.*, p. 419.
14. *Ibid.*, p. 486.

15. *74th Annual Report, 1989,* California Department of Conservation, Division of Oil and Gas.
16. *California Almanac, Fifth Edition,* p. 469.
17. *California Statistical Abstract, 1990,* California Department of Finance.
18. *California Almanac, Fifth Edition,* p. 318.
19. *Venture Capital Journal,* 1990.
20. *California Almanac, Fifth Edition,* p. 317.
21. "Costs Curb Quake Preparedness," *USA Today,* October 16, 1990.
22. "Power of the Pacific Rim," *Los Angeles Times,* May 21, 1991.
23. *Number and Characteristics of Travellers to California,* California Office of Economic Research, 1988.
24. *Ibid.*
25. *Statistical Abstract, 1990,* U.S. National Park Service.
26. *Statistical Report, 1990,* California Department of Parks and Recreation.
27. *California Almanac, Fifth Edition,* p. 346.
28. "California: the trading state," *San Francisco Examiner,* June 18, 1991.
29. *Economic and Business Outlook,* Bank of America, August 1991.
30. *Economic Impact Study of the Film Industry in California, 1988,* California Film Commission.
31. *California Almanac, Fifth Edition,* p. 533.
32. Thom Calandra, "S.F. lags way behind L.A. as Pacific Rim city," *San Francisco Examiner,* September 10, 1990.
33. *Annual Import-Export Study, 1989,* California World Trade Commission.
34. "California—They Paved Paradise," *The Economist,* October 13, 1990.

CHAPTER THREE

1. *Report to the Governor on Labor Market Conditions,* California Employment Development Department, Economic Analysis Group, 1990.
2. "State Expected To Dominate U.S. Job Growth," *San Francisco Chronicle,* June 12, 1990.
3. *Forecast of Economic Activity in the 1990's,* Bureau of Economic Analysis, U.S. Department of Commerce.
4. *California Population Statistics, 1991 Edition,* Center for Continuing Study of the California Economy, Palo Alto, CA, 1991, p. 50.
5. *Ibid.*
6. *California Economic Growth, 1991 Edition,* Center for Continuing Study of the California Economy, Palo Alto, CA, 1991, p. 46.
7. *Report to the Governor on Labor Market Conditions,* 1990.
8. *California Population Characteristics, Special Edition, 1990,* Center for Continuing Study of the California Economy, Palo Alto, CA, pp. 50–51.

9. *Union Labor in California,* California Department of Industrial Relations, 1990.
10. Raymond G. McLeod, "2-Income Families Have Trouble Keeping Up," *San Francisco Chronicle,* August 6, 1990.

CHAPTER FOUR

1. Elizabeth D. Wise, "L.A.'s beautiful freeway paved way for the rest," *San Francisco Examiner,* December 30, 1990.
2. *Ibid.*
3. *Encyclopaedia Americana,* Grolier Incorporated, Danbury, CT, 1990, Vol. 23, p. 565.
4. Interview with Mariana Mejia, Public Affairs Department, California Department of Transportation, October 26, 1990.
5. *California 2000: Gridlock in the Making: Major Issues in Transportation,* Sacramento, CA, Assembly Office of Research, 1988, p. 23.
6. Interview with Reg Hudson, Chief of the Transportation Planning Division, California Department of Transportation, October 23, 1990.
7. *California 2000: Gridlock in the Making,* p. 25.
8. *Energy Watch,* California State Energy Commission, 1990.
9. *California 2000: Gridlock in the Making,* p. 8.
10. Interview with Gordon Hutchins, Chief of the Resource Analysis Branch, California Department of Transportation, Division of Transportation Planning, October 25, 1990.
11. *California 2000: Gridlock in the Making,* p. 25.
12. *California's Aging, Crowded Highways,* The Road Information Program, Washington, DC, 1990, p. 4.
13. *Ibid.,* pp. 5–6.
14. "Judge Halts Expansion of Bay Area Freeways," *San Francisco Chronicle,* December 22, 1990.
15. Elliot Diringer, "Private 'Freeways' An Answer to Full Freeways," *Los Angeles Times,* November 4, 1990.
16. *Ibid.*
17. Bay Area Council Poll on Public Concerns, as reported in the *San Francisco Chronicle,* January 8, 1991.
18. *California 2000: Gridlock in the Making,* p. 9.
19. "French Rail Plan May Be Derailed in Countryside," *Los Angeles Times,* November 6, 1990.
20. "New Network of Fast Trains in Europe," *San Francisco Chronicle,* January 17, 1991.

21. "Japan Starts Work on Supertrain," *San Francisco Chronicle,* November 29, 1990.
22. "A Quick Solar System," *San Francisco Chronicle,* November 12, 1990.
23. "Chrysler Plans Battery-operated Vans," *USA Today,* January 7, 1991.
24. "Paul MacCready Driving Ahead," *U.S. News & World Report,* April 23, 1990.
25. "Smart Way to Unclog Nation's Roads," *Los Angeles Times,* March 30, 1991.
26. Lori Sharn, "Critics Say Triple Trucks Mean Double Trouble," *USA Today,* January 8, 1991.
27. Edward M. Gomez, "Time for the Teeny Tinies?" *Time Magazine,* December 10, 1990.
28. *Annual Report of Fatal and Injury Motor Vehicles Traffic Accidents,* California Highway Patrol, 1989, p. ix.
29. *Ibid.*
30. *Ibid.*
31. "Cars vs. Smog," *San Francisco Chronicle,* October 7, 1990.
32. Elliot Diringer, "A Push to Cut Traffic 35% in Seven Years," *San Francisco Chronicle,* January 16, 1991.
33. Jake Steinman, editor and publisher of *City Sports Magazine,* as quoted in the *San Francisco Examiner,* November 25, 1990.
34. California Department of Transportation, Division of Aeronautics.
35. Martin Halstuk, "Bay Area Airports Plan Big Expansions," *San Francisco Chronicle,* September 4, 1990.
36. *Ibid.*
37. *Outlook for Air Travel in the Twenty-First Century,* National Research Council, National Academy of Sciences, 1990.

CHAPTER FIVE

1. "A Firsthand Look at the School Crisis," *San Francisco Chronicle,* May 6, 1991.
2. *California Almanac, Fifth Edition,* Pacific Data Resources, Santa Barbara, CA, 1991, p. 63.
3. *Ibid.,* p. 70.
4. *California Assessment Program,* California Department of Education, 1989.
5. Ramon G. McLeod, "Baby Boom Threatens Schools," *San Francisco Chronicle,* May 20, 1991.
6. *Fact Sheet, 1990–1991,* California Department of Education, p. 44.

7. *Ibid.*
8. Louis Freedburg, "Schools Struggle to Finance Reforms," *San Francisco Chronicle,* September 18, 1990.
9. *Ibid.*
10. *Fact Sheet, 1990–91,* p. 37.
11. William Trombley, "Huge Bond Issue Would Bring Relief," *Los Angeles Times,* October 13, 1990.
12. *Report by the National Education Association on Teachers' Salaries,* 1991.
13. The Census Bureau and Scripps-Howard News Service, *Report for the 1989 School Year,* June 1991.
14. *California Almanac, Fifth Edition,* p. 63.
15. Thomas Toch, "Putting Students First—At Last," *This World,* November 4, 1990.
16. Daniel M. Weintraub, "Business Gives Public Schools Failing Grade," *Los Angeles Times,* January 24, 1991.
17. "Survival of the Fittest Schools," *Los Angeles Times,* April 18, 1991.
18. W. Dale Nelson, "Classroom news creator plans for-profit schools," *San Francisco Examiner,* May 17, 1991.
19. *Ibid.*
20. Nanette Asimov, "Catholic Schools Try For Comeback," *San Francisco Chronicle,* November 19, 1990.
21. "Educators Embrace National Exam," *U.S. News & World Report,* December 31, 1990.
22. *Fact Sheet,* California Department of Education, 1991, p. 28.
23. Speech to the Republican Eagles by Lamar Alexander, U.S. Secretary of Education, Washington DC, May 9, 1991.
24. *California Almanac, Fifth Edition,* pp. 75–77.
25. *Ibid.*

CHAPTER SIX

1. Marc Reisner, *Cadillac Desert,* Viking Press, New York, 1986, p. 346.
2. *California Almanac, Fifth Edition,* Pacific Data Resources, Santa Barbara, CA, 1991, p. 419.
3. *Economic Indicators of the Farm Sector, State Financial Summary,* U.S. Department of Agriculture, 1990.
4. Maria L. LaGanza, "Drought May Idle 600,000 Acres of Farmland in State," *Los Angeles Times,* March 29, 1991.
5. Maria L. LaGanza, "Drought Spells Big Changes on the Farms," *Los Angeles Times,* February 8, 1991.

6. Dan Nelson, general manager of the San Luis Water District, as quoted in the *Los Angeles Times,* March 29, 1991.
7. Annie Nakao, "State dairy farmers face grim future," *San Francisco Examiner,* February 9, 1991.
8. Interview with Lance Barnett in Sacramento, October 24, 1990.
9. "Freeze toll to crops hits $670 million," *San Francisco Examiner,* January 10, 1991.
10. Nancy Rivera Brooks, "The Great Freeze," *Los Angeles Times,* January 6, 1990.
11. Maria L. La Ganza, "Source of New Citrus Trees in State Damaged," *Los Angeles Times,* January 14, 1991.
12. *Dairy Outlook and Situation,* U.S.D.A. Economics and Statistics Service, 1990.
13. *California Almanac, Fifth Edition,* p. 436.
14. *Ibid.,* p. 444.
15. Robert Giacomini, president of the Western United Dairy Farmers Association, as quoted in the *Los Angeles Times,* February 9, 1991.
16. *California Livestock Statistics,* California Department of Food and Agriculture, 1990.
17. *California Almanac, Fifth Edition,* p. 440.
18. *Ibid.*
19. Vlac Kershner, "Californians Cutting Down On Their Alcohol Consumption," *San Francisco Chronicle,* December 28, 1990.
20. *Ibid.*
21. Anthony Dias Blue, "Bad Bugs," *California Magazine,* May 1991, p. 106.
22. Judy Pasternak, "Pollution Is Choking Farm Belt," *Los Angeles Times,* April 22, 1991.
23. *Ibid.*
24. *Ibid.*
25. Brian Mudd, Director of Air Pollution at the University of California, Riverside, as quoted in the *Los Angeles Times,* April 22, 1991.
26. *California Fruit and Nut Review,* U.S. Department of Agriculture, Washington, DC, 1990.
27. Tom Sietsema, "This Nut Is State's Biggest Food Export," *San Francisco Chronicle,* October 10, 1990.
28. Tom St. John, molecular biologist, Fred Hutchinson Research Center, as quoted in *Megatrends* by John Naisbitt and Patricia Aburdene, William Morrow and Co., New York, 1990, p. 251.
29. *Exports of Agricultural Commodities Produced in California,* California Department of Food and Agriculture, 1990.

30. *Foreign Ownership of U.S. Agriculture*, U.S. Department of Agriculture, Economic Research Service, 1990.
31. *U.S. Census of Agriculture*, U.S. Department of Commerce, Bureau of the Census, 1991.
32. *California Almanac, Fifth Edition*, pp. 422, 443.

CHAPTER SEVEN

1. Marc Reisner, *Cadillac Desert*, Viking Press, New York, 1986, p. 64.
2. David Perlman, "Past Droughts Lasted A Lot Longer," *San Francisco Chronicle*, April 19, 1991.
3. "Drought gives lesson in economics," *San Francisco Examiner*, March 3, 1991.
4. Jane Ganahl, "Why it does or doesn't rain in California," *San Francisco Examiner*, March 8, 1991.
5. "Past Droughts," April 19, 1991.
6. *Environmental Scanning Report*, Strategic Division of Transportation Planning, California Department of Transportation, 1987, p. 44.
7. Elliot Diringer, "California's Plumbing—An Overview of the State's Water System," *San Francisco Chronicle*, April 15, 1991.
8. *Ibid.*
9. *Ibid.*
10. *Cadillac Desert*, p. 379.
11. David Perlman, "Valley May Sink As Well Use Increases," *San Francisco Chronicle*, December 3, 1990.
12. *California Almanac, Fifth Edition*, Pacific Data Resources, Santa Barbara, CA, 1991, p. 130.
13. Robert Gilliom, as quoted in the *San Francisco Chronicle*, December 3, 1990.
14. *Ibid.*
15. *Cadillac Desert*, p. 9
16. Charles C. Hardy, "Plan to create reservoir may go down the drain," *San Francisco Examiner*, January 10, 1991.
17. Poll of California residents taken January 26–29, 1991, as reported in *Los Angeles Times*, January 31, 1991.
18. Dan Martinez, "Rubber comes to the rescue," *San Francisco Examiner*, February 2, 1991.
19. "Who Uses California Water?" *Los Angeles Times*, October 16, 1990.
20. As quoted in *USA Today*, "Cities Thirst For Farmers' Water Rights," February 19, 1991.

21. Miles Corwin, "Are Farms Wasting Water?" *Los Angeles Times*, October 16, 1990.
22. "The State's Water Crisis," *Los Angeles Times*, January 16, 1991.
23. David Perlman, "Desalting Plants May Quench Water Woes," *San Francisco Chronicle*, October 29, 1990.
24. Jane Kay, "Thirsty Cities Look At Desalination," *San Francisco Chronicle*, February 3, 1991.
25. Jenifer Warren, "Catalina Discovers The Ocean," *Los Angeles Times*, June 25, 1991.
26. "Desalting Plants," October 29, 1990.
27. *Ibid.*
28. "How Salt Water Might Some Day Help Slake Thirst," *Los Angeles Times*, February 25, 1991.
29. Miles Corwin, "Town's Rationing Plan—10 Gallons a Person Daily," *Los Angeles Times*, March 7, 1991.
30. Susan Sward, "More Agencies Try Cloud Seeding," *San Francisco Chronicle*, February 21, 1991.
31. *Ibid.*
32. Allan R. Gold, "Drinking Water Will Be Purer, But At What Price?" October 7, 1990.
33. "California Turns Seaward to Slake Thirst For Water," *Los Angeles Times*, February 18, 1991.
34. Maria L. La Ganza, "Goleta Initiates Plan to Import Canadian Water," *Los Angeles Times*, March 13, 1991.
35. *Ibid.*
36. Walt Gibbs, "S.F. may intensify rationing of water," *San Francisco Examiner*, January 25, 1991.
37. Susan Yoacham and Jerry Roberts, "State Has Lived In A Water Fantasy," *San Francisco Chronicle*, March 1, 1991.

CHAPTER EIGHT

1. *California Almanac, Fifth Edition*, Pacific Data Resources, Santa Barbara, CA, 1991, p. 50.
2. "Health Care Costs To Rocket," *Los Angeles Times*, November 1, 1990.
3. *California Almanac, Fifth Edition*, p. 53.
4. Jonathan Marshall, "Health Care Industry Booming," *San Francisco Chronicle*, March 7, 1991.
5. *Ibid.*
6. *California Almanac, Fifth Edition*, p. 57.

7. *Ibid.,* pp. 50, 57.
8. Lisa M. Krieger, "The Cost Of Closing Public Hospitals," *San Francisco Chronicle,* January 3, 1990.
9. Robert Steinbrook, "California Trails U.S. Cancer Rate," *Los Angeles Times,* February 29, 1991.
10. Mike Snyder, "Getting By With A Pin, A Valve . . . ," *USA Today,* February 27, 1991.
11. "A Revolution In Making Babies," *Time Magazine,* November 5, 1990.
12. Doug Podulsky, "Having Babies Past Forty," *U.S. News & World Report,* October 29, 1991.
13. Marlene Cimons, "AIDS: It's Changed Us Forever," *Los Angeles Times,* May 31, 1991; "Box score on AIDS," *San Francisco Examiner,* June 9, 1991.
14. "The health insurance squeeze," *San Francisco Examiner,* October 7, 1990.
15. Jayne Garrison, "Caught in a trap of technology," *San Francisco Examiner,* October 8, 1990.

CHAPTER NINE

1. *Report of 1989,* California Air Resources Board, Technical Support Division.
2. Michael D. Lemonick, "Forecast: Clearer Skies," *Time Magazine,* November 5, 1990.
3. "Tough Anti-Smog Rules Imposed On Consumer Products In State," *San Francisco Chronicle,* October 12, 1990.
4. Richard W. Stevenson, "California To Get Tougher Air Quality Rules," *New York Times,* September 27, 1990.
5. "Air Control Goes Regional," *Los Angeles Times,* April 28, 1991.
6. Barry R. Wallerstein, AQMD Planning Director, as quoted in *Los Angeles Times,* April 28, 1991.
7. Otto Bos, Assistant to Governor Wilson, as quoted in *Los Angeles Times,* December 21, 1990.
8. Interview with Robin Maroze, Research Program Specialist, California Department of Forestry, September 12, 1991.
9. Research Notes, California Air Resources Board, May 1989.
10. *California Almanac, Fifth Edition,* Pacific Data Resources, Santa Barbara, CA, p. 122.
11. Jane Kay, "Farallon Gulf littered with nuclear waste," *San Francisco Examiner,* November 18, 1990.

12. Maria L. La Ganza, "Farms Could Cut Chemical Use, Environmentalists Say," *Los Angeles Times,* May 22, 1991.
13. "Report of Pesticides Sold in California," California Department of Food and Agriculture, 1987.
14. "New technique could replace pesticides," *San Francisco Examiner,* July 5, 1991.
15. "Cleaning Up The Environment," *U.S. News & World Report,* March 25, 1991.
16. "Compost Plan Stirs Up Heap Of Controversy," *Los Angeles Times,* June 18, 1991.
17. Interview with Darice Bailey of the California Department of Health, September 11, 1991.
18. Keay Davidson, "Transmutation to end nuclear waste problem," *San Francisco Examiner,* June 24, 1991.
19. Annie Nakao, "Manure may be used to recycle hazardous waste," *San Francisco Examiner,* May 17, 1991.
20. "Settlement Reached in Rice-Straw Flap," *San Francisco Chronicle,* May 29, 1991.
21. *California Almanac, Fifth Edition,* p. 147.
22. *Ibid.,* pp. 155, 165.
23. "National Parks Paying the Price Of Popularity," *USA Today,* July 8, 1991.
24. "U.S. allocates $39 million to buy California park lands," *San Francisco Examiner,* November 9, 1990.
25. Jane Kay, "Greenways asked along state rivers," *San Francisco Examiner,* January 3, 1991.
26. *Effects of the Drought on the California Economy and Environment,* Pacific Institute for Studies in Development, Environment and Security, Berkeley, CA, 1991.
27. Michael Dorigan, "Growth curbs win big in Half Moon Bay," *San Francisco Examiner,* May 8, 1991.
28. Interview with Sandy Mah of the California Environmental Protection Agency, September 13, 1991.
29. Frank Viviano, "Learning to Live With Toxic Waste," *San Francisco Chronicle,* June 17, 1991.
30. *California Almanac, Fifth Edition,* p. 140.
31. *The Next Big Earthquake,* United States Geological Survey, Department of the Interior, 1990, pp. 14–15.
32. Judy Keen, "Costs Curb Quake Preparedness Programs," *USA Today,* October 16, 1990.

CHAPTER TEN

1. *California Almanac, Fifth Edition,* Pacific Data Resources, Santa Barbara, CA, 1991, p. 88.
2. *Ibid.,* p. 87.
3. *Population Projections, 1990–1996,* California Department of Corrections, Spring 1991, p. 1.
4. *Crime and Delinquency in California, 1980–1989,* State of California Department of Justice, 1990, pp. 10–19.
5. *Ibid.,* p. 20.
6. "Drugs, Small Dealers Get Light Terms," *Los Angeles Times,* December 18, 1990.
7. *Ibid.*
8. *Ibid.*
9. Michael Inikoff, "Survey Finds Drop In Cocaine Use," *San Francisco Chronicle,* December 20, 1990.
10. *Crime and Delinquency in California,* pp. 33–38.
11. *California Almanac, Fifth Edition,* p. 87.
12. John Hurst, "Full Cells and Empty Pockets," *Los Angeles Times,* May 8, 1991.
13. George Will, "The Journey Up From Guilt," *Newsweek Magazine,* June 18, 1990, p. 68.
14. David Dietz, "A Deukmejian Legacy—Expanded Prison System," *Los Angeles Times,* December 17, 1990.
15. "Overcrowding Crisis In State Prisons," *San Francisco Chronicle,* April 22, 1991.
16. Interview with Christine May, Department of Corrections, Sacramento, July 1, 1991.
17. Ann Bancroft, "No Relief In Sight For Overcrowded California Prisons," *San Francisco Chronicle,* April 22, 1991.
18. *Characteristics of Population in California State Prisons by Institution, December 31, 1990,* Department of Corrections, p. 12.
19. *Ibid.,* p. 12.
20. Carolyn Skorneck, "Violent crimes spurt in U.S. rural states," *San Francisco Examiner,* June 10, 1991.
21. *Crime and Delinquency in California, 1990, Advance Release,* California Department of Justice, 1991, p. 3.
22. *Ibid.,* p. 13.
23. *Crime And Delinquency In California, 1980–1989,* State of California Department of Justice, 1990, pp. 9, 99.
24. *Ibid.,* p. 68.

25. Gregory Lewis, "Startling figure on blacks in jails," *San Francisco Examiner*, November 1, 1990.
26. *California Almanac, Fifth Edition*, p. 104; interview with Toni Welch, Supervisor, Firearms and Permits Unit, Department of Justice.
27. Greg Lucas, "Proposal on Semi-Automatic Weapons," *San Francisco Chronicle*, January 16, 1991.
28. *California Almanac, Fifth Edition*, p. 105.
29. Interview with Charlotte A. Rhea, Research Analyst, Office of the Attorney General, July 1, 1991.
30. "No Relief In Sight For Overcrowded California Prisons," *San Francisco Chronicle*, April 22, 1991.

CHAPTER ELEVEN

1. Statement of Norma Flynn of the Los Angeles Philharmonic, November 6, 1991.
2. Statement of Pilar Muñoz of the Museum of Modern Art, November 6, 1991.
3. John Naisbitt and Patricia Aburdene, *Megatrends 2000*, William Morrow and Company, New York, 1990, p. 66.
4. Interview with Kris Saslow, Managing Director of the Association of California Symphony Orchestras, June 17, 1991.
5. *Directory of California Museums*, California Association of Museums, 1990.
6. *California Almanac, Fifth Edition*, Pacific Data Resources, Santa Barbara, CA, p. 533.
7. Interview with Ken Larsen, Associate Director, California Confederation of the Arts, June 17, 1991.
8. *Megatrends 2000*, pp. 76–77.
9. *Directory of California Museums*, a partial listing.
10. *California Library Statistics*, 1990, Library Development Services Bureau, California State Library.
11. Gerald D. Adams, "Classic architectural design for new library elicits raves," *San Francisco Examiner*, October 2, 1990.
12. *Megatrends 2000*, p. 73.
13. Brenda Berlin, "Historic chance for the arts in S.F.," *San Francisco Examiner*, July 13, 1991.
14. *Megatrends 2000*, p. 73.
15. *Ibid.*, p. 84.
16. Bob Pool, "A House In Harmony," *Los Angeles Times*, January 20, 1991.

17. *California Almanac, Fifth Edition,* pp. 351, 359.

18. *Variety,* as reported in The Kiplinger California Letter, August 8, 1990.

19. Kenneth J. García, "Plant Makes Comeback As Film Library," *Los Angeles Times,* January 21, 1991.

20. "Mountain View's Spiffy Arts Center," *San Francisco Chronicle,* December 6, 1990.

21. *Radius,* California Assembly of Local Art Galleries, Fall 1990.

22. *Ibid.,* April 1991.

23. *Ibid.,* May–June 1990.

24. *California Arts Council Anniversary Report,* Sacramento, CA, 1986, p. 8.

25. Interview with Jo Ann Anglin, Information Division, Arts Council of California, October 23, 1990.

26. "Artsfax, The Bay Area Partnership, The Bay Area," The San Francisco Foundation, 1988.

CHAPTER TWELVE

1. Sharon Shaw Johnson, "How The States Have Changed," *USA Today,* December 29, 1990.

2. Ramon G. McLeod, "U.S. Census Shows Big Shift West and South," *San Francisco Chronicle,* December 27, 1990.

3. Kam Kuwata, as quoted in "Super Year For California Politics," *San Francisco Chronicle,* May 2, 1991.

4. Patricia King, "A California Gold Rush," *Newsweek,* April 22, 1933, p. 33.

5. George Gorton, as quoted in *San Francisco Chronicle,* May 2, 1991.

6. Jerry Roberts, "Early Primary Plan Gets a Boost," *San Francisco Chronicle,* May 25, 1991.

7. Sara Fritz and Dwight Morris, "California Cash May Stay Home Next Year," *Los Angeles Times,* June 10, 1991.

8. Paul Jacobs, *Los Angeles Times,* "Term Limits Would Oust Lawmakers and a System," October 13, 1990.

9. David Savage and Richard Simon, "High Court Lets County Redistricting Stand," *Los Angeles Times,* January 8, 1991.

10. Bill Stall, "Political Scramble Expected Over 7 New House Seats," *Los Angeles Times,* December 28, 1990.

Selected Bibliography

BOOKS

Adams, Charles, *Heroes of the Golden Gate,* Palo Alto, CA, Pacific Books, 1987.

Dressler, Fritz and Seybold, John, *The Entrepreneurial Age,* Media, PA, Seybold Publications, 1985.

Dychtwald, Ken, *Age Wave,* New York, Bantam Books, 1990.

Fay, James S., *California Almanac,* Fifth Edition, Santa Barbara, CA, Pacific Data Resources, 1991.

Jackson, Joseph Henry, *Western Gate,* New York, Farrar, Straus and Young, 1952.

Lewis, Oscar, *The Big Four,* New York, Alfred A. Knopf, 1946.

Moskowitz, Milton, *The Global Marketplace,* New York, Macmillan, 1985.

Naisbitt, John and Aburdene, Patricia, *Megatrends 2000,* New York, William Morrow and Company, 1990.

Reiff, David, *Los Angeles: Capital of the Third World,* New York, Simon & Schuster, 1991.

Reisner, Marc, *Cadillac Desert,* New York, Viking Press, 1986

Rosecrance, Richard, *The Rise of the Trading State,* New York, Basic Books, 1986.

Toffler, Alvin, *Power Shift,* New York, Bantam Books, 1990.

Zuboff, Shoshana, *The Future of Work and Power,* New York, Basic Books, 1988.

PERIODICALS

California Magazine, May 1991.

Economic and Business Outlook, Bank of America, July 1988 to Spring 1991.

Los Angeles Times, October 13, 1990–December 13, 1991.

New York Times, June 9, 1990–August 6, 1991.

Newsweek, June 18, 1990–June 17, 1991.

San Francisco Chronicle, August 12, 1989–December 18, 1991.

San Francisco Examiner, May 8, 1989–December 1, 1991.

The Economist, October 13, 1990.

Time Magazine, November 19, 1990–November 18, 1991.

U.S. News & World Report, October 29, 1990 and March 25, 1991.

USA Today, October 16, 1990–January 8, 1991.

JOURNALS AND PAMPHLETS

Agenda for the Twenty-First Century, A Blue-Print for K–12 Education, Sacramento, CA, California State Department of Education, 1987.

Annual Import-Export Study, 1989, Sacramento, CA, California World Trade Commission, 1989.

Annual Report of Fatal and Injury Motor Vehicle Traffic Accidents, Sacramento, CA, California Highway Patrol, 1989.

Artsfax, '86, The Bay Area Partnership, San Francisco, CA, San Francisco Foundation, 1986.

California 2000: A People in Transition: Major Issues Affecting Human Resources, Sacramento, CA, Assembly Office of Research, 1986.

California 2000: Getting Ahead of the Growth Curve: The Future of Local Government in California, Sacramento, CA, Assembly Office of Research, 1989.

California 2000: Gridlock in the Making: Major Issues in Transportation, Sacramento, CA, Assembly Office of Research, 1988.

California Air Quality: A Status Report, Sacramento, CA, California Air Resources Board, 1990.

California Air Quality, Sacramento, CA, California Air Resources Board, 1991.

California Arts Council Anniversary Report, Sacramento, CA, 1986.

California County Projections, 1990 Edition, Palo Alto, CA, Center for Continuing Study of the California Economy, 1990.

California Economic Growth, 1991 Edition, Palo Alto, CA, Center for Continuing Study of the California Economy, 1991.

California Library Statistics, 1990, Sacramento, CA, California State Library, 1990.

California Livestock Statistics, Sacramento, CA, California Department of Food and Agriculture, 1990.

California Population Characteristics, 1991 Edition, Palo Alto, CA, Center for Continuing Study of the California Economy, 1991.

California Population Characteristics, Special Edition, 1990, Palo Alto, CA, Center for Continuing Study of the California Economy, 1990.

California Prisoners and Parolees, 1989, Sacramento, CA, Department of Corrections, 1990.

California Statistical Abstract, Sacramento, CA, California Department of Finance, 1990.

California Transportation Directions, Mobility for 2010, Sacramento, CA, California Transportation Department, 1990.

California's Aging, Crowded Highways, Washington, DC, The Road Information Program, 1990.

Capital Outlay and Infrastructure Report, 1991, Sacramento, CA, State Department of Finance, 1991.

Characteristics of Population in California State Prisons by Institution, Sacramento, CA, Department of Corrections, 1991.

Crime and Delinquency in California, 1990, Advance Release, Sacramento, CA, California Department of Justice, 1991.

Crime and Delinquency in California, 1980–1989, Sacramento, CA, State of California Department of Justice, 1990.

Crime in the United States, Washington, DC, U.S. Department of Justice, 1990.

Criminal Justice Profile, Sacramento, CA, Office of the Attorney General, 1990.

Crop Losses From Air Pollution in California, Sacramento, CA, California Air Resources Board, 1989.

Dairy Outlook and Situation, Washington, DC, U.S. Dairy Association, Economics and Statistical Service, 1990.

Directory of California Museums, California Association of Museums, 1990.

Economic Impact Study of the Film Industry in California, 1988, Los Angeles, CA, California Film Commission, 1988.

Economic Report of the Governor, 1989, Sacramento, CA, Department of Finance, 1989.

Estimates of Refugees in California Counties and the State, 1988, Sacramento, CA, Department of Finance, 1989.

Fact Sheet, 1990–91, Sacramento, CA, California Department of Education, 1991.

Final Report, Meeting the Challenge, Sacramento, CA, California Department of Education, 1990.

Five Year Facilities Master Plan, Sacramento, CA, California Department of Corrections, 1991.

Forecast of Economic Activity in the 1990's, Washington, DC, Bureau of Economic Analysis, U.S. Department of Commerce, 1989.

Foreign Ownership of Agriculture, Washington, DC, U.S. Department of Agriculture, Economic Research Service, 1990.

Historical Statistics of the United States, Washington, DC, U.S. Department of Commerce, 1986.

Homicide in California, Sacramento, CA, Office of the Attorney General, 1990.

Interim Population Projections for California State and Counties, 1990–2005, Sacramento, CA, State of California Department of Finance, 1991.

Number and Characteristics of Travellers to California, Sacramento, CA, California Office of Economic Research, 1988.

Opening Doors, Sacramento, CA, California Department of Education, 1989.

Population Projections for California Counties, 1980–2020, Sacramento, CA, Department of Finance, 1986.

Population Projections, 1990–1996, Sacramento, CA, California Department of Corrections, 1991.

"Profile," A Supplement to Crime and Delinquency in California, Sacramento, CA, Office of the Attorney General, 1989.

Projected Total Population For California By Race/Ethnicity, Sacramento, CA, Department of Finance, 1988.

Radius, Publication of the California Assembly of Local Arts Agencies, Sacramento, CA, Fall 1988 through March 1991.

Smog and California Crops, Sacramento, CA, California Air Resources Board, 1991.

Statistical Abstract, United States Park Service, Washington, DC, 1990.

The Next Big Earthquake, Washington DC, U.S. Geological Survey, U.S. Department of the Interior, 1990.

Transportation in California: Problems and Options Through the Year 2000, Sacramento, CA, Assembly Office of Research, 1987.

Trends Affecting Caltrans, Sacramento, CA, California Department of Finance, 1990.

Ultra Clean: Cars and Fuels, Sacramento, CA, California Air Resources Board, 1990.

Vision California 2010, Sacramento, CA, California Economic Development Corporation, 1990.

Index

ABC (Anywhere But California) syndrome, 219

"Abortion pill" (RU-486), 154

Academy of Motion Picture Arts and Sciences Center for Motion Picture Study, 201

Acquired Immune Deficiency Syndrome (AIDS), 25, 154-56

Afro-American History and Life, California Center for, 195

Agriculture: air pollution, 114-16; almonds and other nuts, 116-17; average farm size, 121; battle for water, 105, 107-10, 122; big freeze of 1990, 110-11; biotechnology, 117-19, 122; California as primary producer, 106-7; California ranking in, 37; California's food exports, 119; cash farm receipts, 105, 122; cattle ranchers and dairy farmers, 41, 109; chemicals and pesticides, 164-66; dairy industry, 111-12; dependence on groundwater, 107; drought and cold weather, 40-41; employment in, 61, 105; foreign ownership of California farmland, 119-20; grapes, raisins, and wines, 112-14; gross income from, 105, 121; livestock industry, 112; number of farmers, 121; problems facing, 41; productivity of California farmers, 121; ranking in cash farm crops, 40; "superbugs," 116; total revenues, 105,

122; use of wells, 128; vegetables, 40; water allocations to, 131-33; water use policy, 109-10, 131-33; wine industry, 40, 113-14

AIDS, 25, 154-56

Air pollution: effect on California agriculture, 114-16; efforts to reduce, 160-62; threat to California forests, 163

Air traffic: increases in, 83-85, 86

Alameda Creek (Fremont): rubber dam on, 131

Alfalfa: effects of drought, 109, 122, 132

Almonds, 106, 116-17

Alta Irrigation District, 107

Amador County: projected growth, 33

American Trucking Association, 79

Anaheim-Santa Ana metropolitan area, 58

Anderson, Harry, 199

Anderson, Margaret, 199

Annenberg, Walter, 199, 203

Arson: incidence of, 189

Art galleries and museums, 194-95

Artichoke farming, 106, 109

Arts: art galleries and museums, 194-95; as a spectator sport, 198-99; as good business, 197-98; ballet, opera, and symphony companies, 193; California Arts Council, 202-3; cultural centers, 201-2; expansion in, 192-93; employment in, 194; ethnic museums, 195-96; libraries, 196-97; major private collections, 199-200; motion picture and television production, 47-48, 194,